Angels in My Way

Angels in My Way

By

Miguel Angel Soto Flores

ISBN 978-0-578-07196-1

FIRST EDITION
Publish and printed in the United States of America.

Table of Contents

Preface

The concept of angels captivated the author since he was a child. Since that time, he has been interested in real life experiences; now, he writes about evidences supporting angels. He wrote this book as an interview between him and a woman, the narrator. This woman explains the reader through her stories the work of her guardian angels. The book reveals real life experiences she had with guardian angels; stories she has collected during more than 50 years starting in her childhood. The reader may learn from her experiences in these stories how the angels accomplished the purpose of her mission.

People believe that God assigns a guardian angel to each one of us to protect and help us with our mission in life. It is comforting to think powerful and invisible agents walk by our sides to care for us all the time. Who would not want to have private bodyguards twenty-four hours seven days a week assigned to care for him or her? The narrator says that one key issue is to know how angels manage circumstances and conditions to achieve desired purposes and results; so, they move our lives towards a final goal, she calls it her mission.

In chapter 1, she states her fears of making public her experiences, and the author discloses the motives he has for writing this book. She also talks about her life during her childhood; she notes that belief is personal and she goes on to confirm her beliefs in guardian angels and spirits. She says she has had her experiences with guardian angels for near her entire life. The author says he knows her for many years and trusts the veracity of her stories; and he goes on to describe her personality at the same time. The book presents her stories in a chronology; it follows her age by phases of her life. In chapter 2, the woman describes the guardian angels' form and looks. She explains how they communicate with us in each stories of her life. The author challenged her beliefs but she argued back to prove them and her experiences in a convincing way; and she goes on to describe what miracle, luck, and destiny are for her. In chapter 3, she tells of her experiences with angels during her childhood years. She explains the risks we have in choosing and making our own decisions. She tells of her studies in a bilingual school she attended. In chapter 4, she tells of the work of the angels during her adolescent years; she suggests we are not in full control of our lives and feels someone else manages our lives. Misti says we go through a natural sequence of events in each phase of our lives; this sequence is beyond our control but in the end, the result is favorable to us. She says in there that we have no control of conditions or circumstances of life. She tells how the angels managed the circumstances and conditions in her stories in more details; they fix the sequence of the events that take us to the end. In chapter 5, she tells of her experiences with angels while living in USA; she tells how they setup links between past and future event for a desired results. She explains how she met a young man that became her permanent companion; she thinks this encounter was the result of the angels work. In chapter 6, she says her angels helped her with finding a job in her native country and explains the drama she went through to marry her boyfriend. She says that her angels setup the conditions to accomplish her wedding and to take her back to USA. In Chapter 7, she tells us her experiences during the time she lived with her husband in America. She says the angels created urgency for her to return to her native country. The reader will find out what was that urgency that she could not ignore. In chapter 8, she tells how the angels changed a hospitable environment to hostile, in a short time. She says she went through violent circumstances in her native country; she says her angels created and managed them. Nevertheless, she says that the violence that squeezed her out of her native country happened for her own good. She thinks that the angels were responsible for the change that in the end expelled her from that country. In chapter 9, the woman tells what she goes through in a neighboring country. She tells how the angels turned that scenario hostile forcing her to get out of that country. This time, she went back to America for good. In chapter 10, she says the United States is a land of miracles; here, opportunities are plenty and dreams come true. She tells how angels helping her to return and how those angels managed the circumstances that helped her settle in this place, in a hurry. In chapter 11, she gives her own conclusions of her stories; at the same time, she offers them her own recommendations to deal with angels' actions. The reader will find out here what she thinks of the concepts, spiritual, and material. The reader will know the details of how angels' pass from their dimension into our world. She gives real evidences of the angels' existence in her stories. She concludes exposing a scheme or synopsis of her life's journey listing her main goals. In chapter 12, the author gives a summary of his notes and gives brief comments of her experiences.

The author thanks the woman for sharing her stories with the readers regardless of fears she could have had. The author thanks the publishing (Lulu's) project team for the assistance and guidance they gave him. He thanks his wife for allowing him the time to produce this book and take it to the reader. The author might not have finished this book without all that help, assistance, and understanding from them. Enjoy!

Chapter 1

Introduction

1 – The Author's Interest in the Subject

I remember the first years of my childhood as if I were living them again. People talked about their deeply seated beliefs in guardian angels; and they still talked about them with respect and passion. Their stories of angels coming in our help opened my desire, as a writer, to study this subject. Their stories frightened and made me apprehensive, but regardless of that, I wanted to hear them. Priests talked about guardian angels during our catechism hours; I liked the theme, though it kept me up thinking of it at night.

I remembered I had met a young woman in a city far away from my hometown few years ago. She told me some of her real life experiences with guardian angels at that time, and that opened my desire to hear more of her stories. I decided to write a book on that subject because now I had the time; and I looked for that young woman who had told me some of her experiences. I found her, and I asked her for an opportunity to hear her stories for a book I wanted to write about her experiences. She accepted and we setup an interview at her house. In this book, I expose real life experiences with guardian angels; this was my interest in writing it. In this book, I give the reader a chance to review the woman's stories; these are a sequence of her real lifetime experiences.

2 – The Interview Setup

When I came to her house, she greeted me and led me to a private studio adjacent to the family room of her house. The furniture arranged in a formal manner with two love seats a sofa lamp and center table. Pictures of her family hang in perfect alignment on the wall; pictures of her children and family members were in a proper setting on these tables. Tables adorned with live plants, orchid, and tulips in glazed ceramic pots. Tall glass windows running along two walls allowed a view of her house cover patio; the deck and courtyard, and large planters designed with seating walls and planted as a typical tropical garden. In fact, she said, "That courtyard is my tropical island. Do you like it?" "Yes, of course," I said. "It is perfect place for relaxing and meditating at any time," I added.

"You have impressed me with the few stories you have already told me. In them, you have revealed the deep understanding you have of the guardian angels issue"; I added to start our conversation. "I am confident that the readers, as I, would like to hear all of your stories, besides the ones you have told me with love and faith. Could you do that for the readers? I will listen with an open mind and more attention to details this time; thus, I may write my book of your real life experiences. I will keep your identification private in this book, but for reference purpose I will call you Misti in my book; is that OK?"I said and waited for her response. Misti had a firm glance at the distance into the courtyard, making a long pause as in deep thoughts, before she answered. She seemed as if she were meditating on the consequences of telling her stories to the public. I waited with patience; however, I hoped to hear a positive answer. I was aware of what that decision meant to Misti; she would let the world into her life, her difficulties, pains, anguishes, and happiness by revealing her beliefs. She turned her head and looked at me at last. Her face showed a candor I have never seen before. I knew that she had reached her decision and was about to tell me.

Misti sighed and said, "Miguel, if we could honor our commitments or promises; and if we could respect the thoughts and beliefs of others, including the belief in guardian angels, we could change our world. If we could respect individual cultures, we would make our world a peaceful place. If we cared more and got along better with each other, we could build a more productive and fair world. The fact is there are ill intentioned people trying to look good and tidy by making others look bad and terrible. They hold an innate selfishness; they think they are always the best and above the rest. Besides that, if we fail to perceive the subtleties of life we reduce our understanding of life. We block our perception with our worries and tribulations, and we fail to perceive the subtleties of life. We receive blows, and upsets, even from loved ones, that often have an effect on our beliefs.

"Sometimes, we think we live with no hope abandoned in this valley of tears we called earth. We might perceive that material ambitions and desires drive us through our life in this world. This world is full of attitudes that reduce our sharing and caring. These attitudes block the delicate and subtle messages that life gives us; and we go on ignoring there is another world full of beauty, love, and compassion. God gave us the world without asking, teaching us that life is more than the anguishes that worries us." Misti paused for a few minutes as if she wanted to collect her thoughts, and said; "I have some apprehensions for which I should keep my experiences off the public, because; indeed I would expose my beliefs to unjust people's conjectures and critics. I should let my stories sleep on the integrity of my faith; I should not wake them up to a shocking unjust and sarcastic reality." She spoke as if she wished to stay out the subject, digressing in her monologue, while maturing her decision. As a writer eager to begin his notes, I was being egoistical wishing that the world knew of her experiences in my book. I admit that I had doubts of my agnostic position. Perhaps I wanted to prove somehow that Misti's angels were real. I wanted to lead her to speak about her life at childhood to get into the subject, and I asked,

"Do you remember your childhood years, Misti?"

She sighed and said, "The simple life of yesteryears, up to when I was a teenage girl, had fewer risks than it has now," she said taking her time. "Everything went by much slower and calmer than in current time. The neighbors were real neighbors, and they knew each other. They cared for each other's problems, sicknesses, joys, and sadness and we did the same to correspond."

"What did you do for entertainment?" I asked.

"We had little contact with the world. Talk radio shows and news were our main broadcasting media during those days. We heard music, spoken tales, and novels through radios. My father, uncles and cousins heard play by play of their favorite sports, as baseball, on radios. I had a record player to play my long play records. I liked big-band music as that of Glenn Miller and others. Local orchestras came to the plazas and played or gave concerts for the people in the weekends. The churches honored their saints each year with festivities and processions in the streets.

"I had fun and enjoy myself during my childhood and adolescent years; I went to parties, dances, and celebrations. I went with anyone of my grandmothers or my father to movie theaters; we walked to cinemas that were close by and sometimes we drove to other more distant cinemas. We went to mass on Sundays; the families, all dressed up, and the people walked around on the church atrium before the mass, happy. The women and young girls wore hats, shawls covering their hair, and heads. I remember those long sermons and readings on christian faith and morals."

"And what about supplies and produces?" I asked, and she continued.

"During those days, we grew, harvest our produce in our farms; we were an agricultural country. We had a country that was not industrialized; we had to import most products, but we manufactured some products by hand for local consumption. Our reward for that was that our life was easy going and calm ideal for a daydreaming." Misti sighed; she seemed trapped in her memories and continued. "Our life was intimate, full of warmth and affection, of honesty and friendship. We live a romantic life in a beautiful place where the air was clean and fresh with fragrance of gardens, and the sky was blue and clear; it was a natural and colorful tropical scenario. I remember when we received the first black and white television set, it surprised the world; it was something exceptional that changed the course of life, since that time. Life was as a mother who cared for her children, in all the homes of all the places."

"What can you tell us about your family conditions during those days?" I asked.

"My parents told me much later that I had born at the end of the Second World War. My family was well to do and conservative; I grew up in that environment. I remember how my mother dressed me up when we went visiting relatives, friends, or neighbors. She felt proud when someone stopped her on the street and praised her for the gracious, girl walking by hand at her side. I grew up with my brother, Marcus, one year younger and my baby sister, Ana, seven years younger than I was. I got my grade school education in a private catholic school; with it, I got also my beliefs in guardian angels. I learned good manners and respect for others, specially the elders."

"Do you believe in God?" I asked her.

"Of course I believe in God." She emphasized. "I believe in the Saints and the souls in penitence, and the guardian angels. I think that souls falling short in their balance of peace with the Lord at the time they departed maintain ties with this world. They wander about in repentance for their sins and sorrows until they pay for them, untying their links. I pray to God and the Virgin Mary so they give their mercy and forgiveness to these souls in penitence, and they may rest in eternal peace. My parents taught me that each one of us has a guardian angel that always walk next to us protecting us. Yes, I believe that, and on several occasions, I have felt as if someone was watching me, have you had an experience like that? I have had strong and clear experiences in my life that confirm the existence of the guardian angels."

"Do you remember all of your experiences with the angels in your way?" I asked. Misti paused for a few seconds and said,

"My experiences have been material and so vivid that I may say they were real. These experiences impressed me much that when I remember them, I see them the same way as when I had them for the first time; but I admit these experiences gave me fear because of their uncertainties or my ignorance of the purpose of their appearance. These experiences were about circumstances and events of which I did not have prior knowledge. They happened in a natural sequence of causal events out of my influence and control; and they will remain in my mind and in my faith as they came, vivid, certain, and complete with their messages."

"What are these experiences for you, Misti?"

"I saw the circumstances making up an event; and I saw, at the same time, the results, and consequences of each event happening for a definite purpose. My experiences focus on the link of events in the journey of my life rather than the circumstances making up an event. This is because the results are the driving element taking me to the end of my mission. My experiences are real life events that happened during my conscious hours. They were no dreams, which I remembered when I woke up. They were real visions and sounds, in the physical scenario where I lived. I know that these experiences with angels and their actions give us fear and apprehensions. In fact, we neither can see nor we can touch the guardian angels; they are spiritual entities. I think that physical tools and methods are not good enough to prove spiritual experiences, are they?"

I said, "Misti, it may not be fair to you, but people would demand physical evidences."

"I observe the actions of powerful entities whose presence I feel but I do not see. I only see their intention in the results of the events they manage. Although I have no record of these experiences, the results of the events prove the angels intentions; these experiences are signs of angels' love and care for us, as I say in my stories. I ask, can we say that they are real when the results of their actions are real?"

Misti paused meditating on her last question. I knew she had a valid point.

"What about the guardian angels, Misti, do you know when they come?" I asked.

"For me, an angel's presence is as if someone, of whom I only see actions and results, tries to communicate with me. They try to tell me something that, I sometimes do not understand in full. They warn or prevent me of something about to happen; they guide me towards it in some occasions, and in others, in an opposite direction to something that may hurt me. The angels act at a precise time in the sequence of events, and that precision surprises me."

"Can you verify their messages?" I prompted her.

"I think I can confirm the validity of those messages at the end of each experience. Let me point out that one may say that these messages are premonitions based on my previous knowledge; however, that is false because I read the messages in the result of a concluding event. Do we have knowledge to see the future to manipulate objects and subjects? We may not have, and we can only speculate hoping that our predictions are correct. The angels set their purposes in a dimension we have no means to access and study their actions; we can predict neither their purposes nor their actions. Studying the effect of my experiences took most of my time and efforts. Besides, for me, the results of the events of these experiences were the key factors of the journey of my life. I accepted my experiences the way they come, and I kept them in my memory for me alone."

"Do you want to tell your stories?"

"Miguel, I know that people can mock my experiences with their opinions. Some appreciate this subject others dislike it, and some others ignore it, that is a fact. I am confident that many persons have had experiences like mine; and even though they may not tell them, we can no longer think of them as fantasies, delusions, or product of beliefs. These experiences are real, and we should observe them to confirm the angels' actions; after all, we only receive love, protection, and benefits from them. They do not come to harm us in any way. Miguel, I think I will tell my experiences for your book in a clear way; but I want to make sure you understand that my intention is to tell my stories about the angels' presence and actions. The readers should trust their own experiences with angels and reason them out; then, they should align their beliefs in angels in accordance with their experiences. I hope that your book can give other persons the courage of telling their own experiences. I would enjoy reading about their experiences because they would support my own as mine would support theirs. Besides, if they tell their stories, we may build greater credibility in the world. I am sure that the more stories we publicize, the more we understand and the more we accept these experiences. Even you, Miguel, may share your stories. I feel that you may have stories of your life that you could share. Perhaps something came out in your favor that you did not expect and made you wonder why. This is the clue; something that happened for your own good outside of your awareness."

"Can anyone prove the angels existence?" I inquired.

"We may study and analyze the experiences that many persons, besides me, have had; however, we are not able to prove them in scientific terms. These experiences are reality in the lives of those who had them; and for each one of them, their experiences will remain with them unproved. I will tell my stories, and in the process, I will explain my understanding of their fundaments. You may help me reason their purposes with your technical knowledge and words. Perhaps we shed light into the proof of the angel's existence."

"How long have you been having these experiences?"

"Let me say, I have had and collected these experiences throughout my entire life since I was six or seven years old."

"Are you afraid to tell your experiences to the public?"

"I have told some of my stories to persons in trust, but to those who believe and understand the same as I do. I said before, there are agnostics who mock stories of the experiences with angels. I do not like mockery or sarcasms of any subject, including the subject of faith. If they mock my stories, I would feel as an illusory person. It makes me feel as though I made up stories to hide a faint personality.

"Have you heard anyone mocking the angels?" I asked her.

"Oh yes, Miguel, I have seen and heard how some people mock these stories and the persons who tells them." She sounded serious and annoyed; perhaps, she was thinking about that kind of people but she continued. "I believe I have a solid character, and if I tell my experiences, it is because I had them." She said in a serious manner. "I know there are individuals who reject the stories of spirits or angels. With their rejection, they may lose connections with entities in that spiritual plane that they long for."

"Do you believe in spirits?" I asked her to change that annoying issue, and she said.

"Yes, I believe in spirits as I believe in God and Heaven. I know that most religions preach of a life after death in a paradise full of love and eternal peace. They say we reunite with relatives, friends, acquaintances and the rest that have gone there at last. We think that they see and hear us, and they know what we do and protect us. Why can there be no souls coming back to this world with a guardian angel mission to care and guide other souls through good paths? I believe in that because I have lived my experiences; and as I had them, I can tell them."

Our dialog started filled with her doubts and apprehensions; it was solemn and gloomy, but she accepted to tell her experiences. I suggested her name to be Misti in this book to keep and safeguard her privacy. I give a fictitious name to each person mentioned in this book to protect his or her identity. As a writer, I want to interpret her experiences with angels and the way she describes her stories. I keep my opinions and thoughts out of the stories of her experiences in all ways or forms. I will help her with my reasoning and words explaining her intentions. I know Misti for many years; I have been in the places where she had her experiences. Therefore, I certify her honest and serious character, trusting her truthfulness.

3 – Let Me Introduce Misti

Misti is a sensitive person with a firm character since her childhood years. She is discreet, obedient, and keeps close to her heart private issues she wants to protect. Misti believes that justice is a sacred right of all that should not be bought as a simple commodity.

She thinks that those who hurt or humiliate someone else do not deserve to be a member of the human race; those actions would not represent love, kindness, and sharing as God intends. Her philosophy is that a person is because of being and not for having. The rule to what makes an individual should not be wealth, but rather the quality of being.

Her keen sense of harmony, of lines, colors, proportions, and balance show up in the decorations of her own house. She strives for perfection, but she knows that perfection is nothing more than a mirage. She likes things done once and right because errors and omissions are permanent things that will bother her while these exists. Perhaps she learns to live with those errors, but she will always reject them. Misti loves the truth; she lives by it and advocates it, because falseness violates the desire of perfection that makes her different. For that reason, she scorns policies based on false promises deceptions and lies. Misti is a friend when she gets to be a friend, trusting and giving everything she can within her sincere friendship. She forever turns off her friendship with no return when she discovers falseness in it. She advocates fairness between persons and she believes that one should cause no loses or pain to other. She has a mindset that makes her susceptible to the delicate actions of the angels. That is the reason that although I may disagree with her beliefs, I respect her and trust the veracity of her stories.

4 – The Chronological Order of her Stories

We agreed to write her stories in five chronological stages of her life; these stages are childhood, adolescence, life as single, and her married life. She told her experiences in each story of each stage progressively according to her age. An event progressed into the next event, building a continuous chain, and a past event served as stepping-stone to current events in that chain. The actions of the angels showed their purpose in the results of each event in that chronology. Her life advances towards the end of her journey with the results of the events accomplished in each phase. The chronology ends when her last story catches up with the present.

Chapter 2

Meet Misti's Angels

1 – Look and Form of Misti's Angels

"Misti, can you tell us the aspects of angels before beginning your stories? I think we will better understand the details of your experiences, is that OK?"

"Yes, Miguel, I will set the fundamental basis of each story."

"Let me ask, Misti, who are the guardian angels? Please, explain how they look, what forms they have, and how and when they show themselves to you. Can you do that for the readers?"

"Miguel, people give the angels an image that is according to their thoughts and beliefs. For some, the angels are cherubs or winged children representing love and caring. Angels look as in the images we see in churches, in paintings or pictures, and the effigies in the stores. I have read in the Bible that God has used angels to send messages and instructions to prophets and apostles. God is the supreme commander, and the angels are soldiers organized by ranks in that line of authority; God gives them assignments they execute in our world. This belief may be true; but, for someone to know about this organization, he or she must have witnessed that system in operation and have returned to report on it. I agree with some authors in one issue, and that is that the guardian angels are God's messengers. I say that because I have seen the angels' entire operation to help us and guard us, and that is a message of love. I noticed that most people envision the angels barefooted and dressed in light colored or white long gowns. My parents told me that a guardian angel was always with me; and after praying at bedtime, my angel guarded my sleep during the night. They might have adopted the belief in angels to instill confidence in their children, but this is not proof of their existence; I have had many real-life experiences that prove their existence. I have read the angels' messages and have seen the execution of their actions. I narrate these experiences in my stories and explain the results of the angels' efforts.

The angel's messages and actions that I tell in my stories debunk doubts of agnostics that say that 'what we believe may not be what it is'. What I tell in my stories is not what counts, but the completed real events and their results. My experiences confirm my faith and beliefs, and I think your book requires that as evidences. I will tell my experiences in each story; in addition, I will explain them with factual details and analysis."

"Would you say your angels exist?"

"By my experiences, I am sure guardian angels exist and take care of us. I am not willing to accept the angels' image people believe they have. We must redefine the guardian angel term to include any form they take, their work plan and real actions so we may prove their existence. Angels take on various forms according to the situation that prompts them to come. The angels take control of the circumstances and adjust the flow of these to achieve an objective. The angels are invisible; they have power, and they are capable of exerting it on objects and subjects. Their force is like the electrical energy that we know. Angels may appear in one case, although the same angel may play different roles using different forms in one case. I will identify and define each angel acting in each story. In my life, I have seen that not everything have been candy and roses for me. Sometimes, I faced adverse situations, as you will hear in my stories. Nevertheless, I am happy to have seen the angels in my way cared for me and protected me always with success. The angels used various ways to give their messages and help when I needed to make a choice or a decision.

"There were situations when the results of their actions missed the goal they targeted. I was distracted and missed their message, or I took it after the event. The angels did their work well. My lack of attention to their messages is always the source of the failure of their plan. Angels make no mistakes; we do. They intervene when we make errors; they adjust the circumstances to offer only the choice to make the proper decision."

"How do angels express themselves?" I asked.

"Angels act through our friend's deed, some stranger's deed, or an animal action when or where we least anticipate. They act with a shock or with a subtle action. They capture our attention stopping us; they alter the flow of circumstances that lead us to the end of an event. They change the timing of the circumstances enough to change the result of an event. The causality of a change of circumstance to its result yields a purpose. Changes in a circumstance part of a set that creates an event yield results different from those the same but undisturbed set yields. An event must meet a set of circumstances or conditions for it to happen; that is, within the tolerance of a desired result. Once that event ends, its result remains forever in the past. The results may be answers to my questions, or an action that can save or the end my life. I mentioned in my stories that I observed subtle signs of a silent language. I concluded that the angels sent these signs to alert me about something that was about to happen. I have received these signs in various occasions. I know my guardian angels revealed themselves and talked to us by way of messages, happenings, and, in this form, they guarded me on time."

"How do your guardian angels look like? How they show themselves?"

"As I have mentioned, the guardian angels, for me, do not have a single face or body; they are not winged young boys or girls dressed in white. Angels may be anything, living thing or any person. An angel can manifest in the action of a dog crossing my path before I took my last step from the sidewalk curb to the street. That dog forced me to stop at the precise moment that a speeding vehicle drove over the point of the step I did not take. I think that in this case, my angel used that dog to prevent me of that imminent danger; the angel changed the order of my activities and my decision of taking that final step, saving me from a sure accident or death. Who could say that my angel did not take the form of a dog at that moment, saved me and then disappear? In another case, the angel could have been the chauffeur of a taxi taking a passenger late to an airport. The passenger lost the flight, and later learned the plane plunged into the sea killing all passengers. This case brings some questions; why was that taxi driver late? Why did they leave the passenger behind? Who decided to save the passenger and why? It is not easy, after seeing the results, to believe that it was luck. I thought about the purpose of that result; I thought about the things or deeds the passenger can do in his or her remaining life; something that otherwise he can no longer do had this passenger boarded that plane.

"I often got feelings that something is going to happen without my looking or thinking for them. These feelings may be the guardian angels' signs trying to tell me something. I have learned to look for and study these signs for many years."

"Can you tell us how the angels get in touch with you?"

"In fact, angels do not get in touch with us. They come when we get out of the path to our mission. People say that there are persons who can communicate with spirits. A medium induced in a trance calls a spirit and the spirit talks through the medium. Communication with spirits proves that there is life after death. I have been in risk facing situations in my life many times, and for some reason, someone notifies me in time. I think that someone is one of my angels caring for me. It may be a stranger who appears and offers me the exact help when I need it, and continues on its way after that. I have some stories about strangers helping me when I needed help; but we may talk about these experiences in other occasion. I believe that angels are energy; I believe angels send their messages by energy impulses that excite atoms in matter or cells in the brain. I have noticed that when something distracts my mind my susceptibility reduces and blocks the angels' signals.

"The guardian angels in my way have neither confirmed faces nor bodies. They take a form that matches the requirements of the circumstances of an event. It is worth the effort hearing the angels' messages in their silent language. The angels talk in their language to those who are attentive to their messages. Those with low susceptible may miss part of these messages; but an agnostic does not hear or ignores these messages. The silent language is the sign language of nature; it is hard to understand, but the angels use it to send their messages. These messages alert us of an event that could happen if the circumstances are not changed. Angels managed the circumstances in my path, objects, and subjects in them, to reach the objectives of my mission. The angels lead our minds to thoughts with their powerful energy; moreover, these thoughts spur us to act. Perhaps the guardian angels move at a high speed that we cannot see; we cannot see them as physical objects because the angels are spirits. Some say to have seen them as silhouettes in rare light. Those of us who study the circumstances of an event can read the angels' messages and can see their actions. That dog's message, for instance, with its unexpected action said, 'Stop, watch out for that vehicle.' I mentioned that, according to my experience, my angels are not on duty twenty-four hours in a day, seven days of every week; no, to me, they appear in circumstances when I need their help."

"Can you call your angels in your way?" I asked.

"No, I do not know of any direct line of communication with the angels. Most people pray as I do, thinking the angels hear and answer them. I am sure that when we yearn for something we transmit signals to the Cosmo that my guardian angels catch, and they work to solve that situation. We must yearn with a humble and vehement attitude, resigned to receive nothing of what we hoped for; and the angels make that something to appear. The exact timing of the result or answers to my yearnings surprises me. The guardian angels catch distress signals, it seems, and at their pace; they work to satisfy our yearnings until they answer or come to help us. I have been in circumstances with neither a possible way out nor where to obtain help to resolve my situations; but always, I received something that got me out of that situation. It may be my positive way to see life; but I have seen how my angels have solved my situations without my participating in the resolution. I have seen the action of the angels when my mind and body was relaxed and calm, patient, at the time of their action; and this state influenced my ability to communicate with the angels. I concluded that a humble yearning in a peaceful state of mind becomes magnet that attracts what I yearn for."

"Could the results be product of coincidences?"

"Of course not, one can deny a result and say it is coincidence; but coincidences happen out of our control in a random mix by chance. However, when we change the circumstances that make up the event for a purpose, its result is not coincidental. One may say that it is luck; it is like wining a lottery with one chance in one hundred million possibilities. In fact, the change of the circumstances making up an event is what modifies not only the result but also its probability; it is not luck showing at the end of the event. I see that the coincidences in the result of a concluded event, but not before. I know that all circumstances making up an event, which has a purpose, satisfy that purpose; the result of that event includes concurrent conditions, they are product of random coincidences, but part of that result. That is the reality of my stories; we live on the edge of risk, a chance in one hundred million possibilities. That is almost a miracle."

"What is a miracle?"

"Some say a miracle is God's intervention; others think it is a break of the laws of nature. For me, a miracle is a happening when it was near impossible. It could be an event without a chance to occur, but the angels manage the circumstances to get the result they want.

"Is it possible?"

"Yes, it could be possible. Angels are messengers carrying out God's instructions; but God could deliver the messages and results

Himself to us instead of the angels, on the one hand. On the other, someone may say that we live on the brink of risk, subject to circumstances in a probabilistic world; and we have no control over random sequence of events or results. Let me say this, if we observe random events, we may notice they present or display undefined purpose. These events happen despite of the consequences of their results. I say that chance is chaotic; it is like a loose hose excited by the energy of the running water that makes it swing without a purpose in whatever direction. This hose can wet whatever is near it with no intention."

"Could it be luck?"

"No, I have mentioned details of a purpose in the action of that dog that made me avoid my last step to my death. How I can say that luck prevented my accident. It was OK for me to cross the street, and I did not expect that speeding car to pass. The dog was not part of my activities to cross the street; but it came unexpected, and it altered my actions. The sequence of the activities leading to that result was not a coincidence; it had an objective, saving my life. This is why I say, luck is a result with no intent to harm or benefit who receives it. Truth highlights this causality: if that dog had arrived at a second slower, I would not have had its disturbance, and I would have taken my last step to death. It is that precision in timing of the angels' actions that astonish me scares and frightens me. Perhaps someone would have screamed," 'It's a miracle.' "And I would have said, 'why that dog, or why me?' For what reason, they saved me from death. Was that out of the generous action of the guardian angels protecting me; is luck a favoring result for me? That is impossible; luck is a random result. It has neither definite purpose nor favors anyone, and we have no control over its occurrence. God granted us free will, freedom to choose, but I see we live in a world of random events hoping for a lucky shot when we make our choices or decisions. I have often heard people saying that each one of us have a mission in this life, and when something happens, as in the case of the dog saving my life, it is for some reason. Perhaps the purpose of life is to accomplish that mission that they know, but we do not, and that is the reason why they manifest and act in a proactive manner as they do. I cannot say that my decisions on the circumstances of an event can give the result I want every time; because, a condition that I did not consider may frustrate the success of that event."

"Would you say this is destiny?"

"Maybe at the end of all stories that mission is the destiny of which we spoke much. The destiny, in fact, is the fulfillment of that mission in the best possible way we manage. If this were true, the actions and decisions we make in life are within our freedom of choosing as long as we follow the course of the mission trusted to us. If the circumstances change my path or I lose the way, the angels come, modify the circumstances, change the results of the events, and put me on course to the end of my journey. For that reason, I say that the angels' purpose is to take care of me in order that I can accomplish the mission. We are unaware of the mission they assigned us, 'do we have to know it?' Let me see; if I did not have any allotted mission any result of my events in my life would be the same for me. We could certainly say that the results are part of our destiny, and we have no choice other than accepting any result. I think that if I have a pre assigned mission I want to participate in the actions that take me to fulfill it. I like to think that I am part of a defined plan rather than taking whatever it comes, when it comes. If we do not participate, we live as dry leaves at the mercy of capricious winds that blow them when or where the winds blow. We are souls of will and purpose in life, and it would be a pity and shameful for us to live with no purpose, as dry leaves in the winds. If we could not choose at all and accept a random world, we would be like puppets subject to the whim of those who pull the strings to simulate our movements. It would be a pity; however, that would not be destiny either. Destiny is a final point, a goal, or harbor to where life takes us whether we wanted or not. Nevertheless, we may not have an apparent mission in life, and we go unburdened through life. In that case, my ultimate mission or destiny is death. Death is our inevitable going away from this physical world to the spiritual realm where we came from."

"What forms do the angels take?"

"Well, my angels manifest in many forms; and knowing they are around me, I study the silent language they use to communicate with me. Thus, I am able to see them in their actions. I know that adverse situations may occur at any time, and I observe the situations around me; however, I know that my angels come to intervene in our favor. I see the body and face of my angels reflected on the meaning of their messages and in the results of their actions. Their messages and actions focus on protecting and caring for us; this is the intention of God, and we should not be afraid to receive that. I received these messages in a language I could not understand well; they hid in the natural occurrence of life. We must leave an open window in our souls so that the guardian angels' energy may enter through it; perhaps we gained more than we lose. If we lose, we just lose our pride of rejecting these guardian angels, disregarding that they come here to protect us."

"Misti, it seems that the deeper we go the more things we need to know, Can you explain this?"

"That is the way it is; we always end up with more questions about the causes behind the choices we make to change the course of our lives. The reasons of my decisions or choices are even more intriguing than those questions. I always stop to think if I had done that instead of this, perhaps it would be other than what it is. If I had taken another choice, what would the result be; what would my life and the life of those around me be if I had decided or taken another way? We all live tied in a positive interdependence; what happens to me affects for sure everyone else in the group. I observed that a group of people moves with me and help me to accomplishing my mission. I have no doubts that an Absolute Intelligence prepares objects and subjects for what comes ahead in our lives; all that outside of my awareness. I could explain why I say 'a group,' but I will let this subject for another occasion. Just let me say that these people are souls traveling together with me in the course of life. Perhaps we have common objectives within a grand master plan that includes the missions assigned to me and them."

"Do you know the communication channels they use?"

"The angels use the circumstances, conditions, to talk to us and the results of events reveal their intent in the end. Those who do not see how causality works miss the opportunities to see the purpose of causes; in other words, they miss the dependency that exists between a cause and its effect. For instance, words are cause and actions are their consequences. The words we speak carry conventional meaning that we collect from their sound waves. The meaning is an energy that excites a combination of brain cells of the listener that moves him or her to act."

"Can you explain how that energy works?"

"I have no technical experience, but let me explain in my way. The people hear the words; they interpret and translate these words into relative meanings, because they do not capture the complete intent of the speaker. Those listening build their own composite meaning of the intent of the speaker, and this meaning incite them to act for good or bad.

"Angels give their messages with the energy of love and care, and their action or force influences the state of both mind and matter. Why should we afraid of the angels? I let them come whenever they need to; I welcome them. The angels as my words are nonmaterial elements of expression. They have neither weight nor volume, but they have energy. This energy can move a mountain, an entire scenario, a dog into action, or incite a thought in my mind; what is the difference? My words are sound waves and the angel's spiritual manifestations; but they are both energy. Look, my words move the air and enter through the ear as sound waves; but their meanings ride on the sound wave. The brain translates these meanings into commands to take a physical action."

"As the angels, does the meaning of my words belong in that dimension where there is no matter?"

"We know that spiritual life is a poorly studied concept. In my stories, I talk about how the angels' actions affected the physical events in my life. I have said that the energy of the angels and of the words, transcend into action by way of their interacting with our world. I have seen the angels at work interacting with our world, as I tell in my stories. This is also the case of the words. Words transcend from the realm of thoughts, which are ethereal and become actions in the physical world. What is the difference? I assert that the subject of my stories is genuine, and I tell my stories for discussion and exchange."

"Misti, do you mean that nothing produces something?"

"No, I do not; I said that life is about thoughts to actions, and it is hard to accept that something we cannot perceive could produce something we do. For instance, we do not see the electrical energy, but it has a capacity to do work which we see. Perhaps, we should consider the spirits as a form of energy with a capacity to do work. I am a normal person who studies the circumstances that happen around me. I analyze the basis and consequences of the events; and I try to explain them in straightforward language. I do not want to make an impression of being a clairvoyant, medium, or psychic. I tell my real-life experiences in my stories, and these are not weird, psychic, or paranormal. They are about spiritual entities that many people believe in. Thus, by observing is how I have been able to understand the actions of my angels throughout my life. I know that our angels act for a definite purpose on our behalf and protection. Furthermore, they act to set a base and support for something else that is to happen in the future. Angels work weaving an embroidering of the events in my life; they leave open certain results of these events waiting to tie in with the new results of future events. This embroidering draws a unique design of the mission of our lives in living colors and forms. Each waiting result is as a yarn they weaved in the embroidering that they will tie, fasten, and support with another thread they will weave ahead. All the yarns, knots and moors, colors forms and drawing they do are part of the embroidering. I believe in the law of cause and effect; I think any action or event happens in order that one or more actions or events can occur ahead. The causality law indicates that an effect has a cause. A cause serves as a base for its posterior effect, independent of the time gap between the cause and its effect. We may fail to see the connection of a cause and its effect due to the subtlety of that connection, on certain occasions. I have showed a clear connection between angels' messages and the vast purpose of my life in the stories I tell. I have seen that events happening in my stories served as a base and support of other events, which occurred in the future. One thing is certain; we cannot see the future circumstances and events around our lives. We cannot see either the mooring of our present, past and, future events. I therefore accept that God executes the plan of my life by way of the angels in my way. I see that all the things coming together outside my control and in my favor take me to a predetermined end. I feel I must participate in the weaving or help threading each knot and moors in the network of the embroidering of my life. In fact, I try to catch the angel's messages to understand them; so, I may then collaborate in the weaving the embroidering of my life. I think, Miguel, I have answered your doubts; I have answered the questions you made in the beginning. I give them with the intention of transmitting my description of what the angels in my way are for me. The angels are transcending energy or force that reach our world and can change the results of physical events. This is my explanation of the actions of the angels in anyone's way. You may go onto analyze the activities of the angels with what I have given you."

"Misti, do you see a definite pattern in the actions of your angels?"

"Yes, Miguel, and I will explain their behavior in my stories; for the moment let me say that we must observe how the result of an event is necessary for future results. For me it is important to find the links between an event and a successor event. These linked events form the network of the embroidering I have mentioned. I have seen how the angels have managed the circumstances to advance the master plan of my mission. Circumstances may disrupt the timing and content of that master plan's as a function of the time and actions of my life. Of course, the angels know the circumstances and conditions of the events and the results that get me closer to my mission. Based on their knowledge, the angels rush or slow down their activities to help me accomplish my mission."

Chapter 3

Angels Came During My Infancy

1 – Who Manages Your Life?

"Misti, you hinted that it is not you who chooses and makes decisions for yourself, is that true? Can you explain that?"

"Miguel, I think that nobody is in full control of his or her decisions. For instance, my life has been less than roses and candies because, I have always lived following orders and choices made by others; and that includes my parents, and my friend's aunt with whom I lived some time, my husband, the circumstances and even of the angels in my way. I think that my life would be different from what it is if I have had complete freedom of choice, my free will. I have been, I am now, and I will be unable to decide what I want on my own. In fact, I have made decisions to satisfy other people, my parents, my husband, my children, and my friends; and in some occasions, even others decide for me. I now make my decisions process to include the welfare of others; I replaced my selfishness with my altruism in that process."

"How do you see yourself in this decision making process?"

"I see myself as a stream running down in a valley carved before beginning my flow and from which I cannot get out to carve my own valley. Life flows in a channel changing its speed according to the inclination or the level of that channel. If the inclination of that channel is steep, life goes fast and if the channel level is flat life flows slowed and relaxed. I found that I could not go outside of that channel for there is always something blocking my desires and decisions. That something returns me to that pre carved valley always. I understand that the angels create that something that blocks my desires. I have seen that the angels' intentions do not agree with mine sometimes, and I often feel as if they take me by the hand along the way, and make choices for me. I know that the angels look out for my best interest, but I want to make my personal choices and decisions; and I wonder, 'does not everybody wants to make their own choices?' I learned living the importance of making my own decisions with my parents; I learned to wait to decide with my own judgment. I think it is not a smart thing to be too sensitive presuming that I should be who directs my fate. I think that is safer to let the angels guide me because they know what is best for me and work for my best interest. Perhaps I should avoid wishing I should be who choose what I want in life. Perhaps, I could ignore that ancient question, 'why am I in this life for'; because if I know I have an assigned mission in my life, and I protected by the angels, I should not worry about my journey. I know that this question express our desire to know the definite purpose we have in life. I know that doing what we want is an erratic endeavor because we do not know if our decision will actually yield what we want. Having a definite purpose in our lives; therefore, does not support doing what we want, because our desires may not conduct us to accomplish our mission. In fact, we see the result of our actions and decisions at the conclusion of the event; therefore, I say that living subject to our actions and decisions is dangerous. The risk we take is that the result may not be what we wanted, and then it would be too late for us to correct the decisions or actions to produce the desired result. My experience has been that when I made a mistake, I have seen that I live with my error and the consequences thereof the rest of my life. Making my own choices and decisions is as if I tried to strike a piñata with blindfolds not knowing if I will hit and break it; obviously, ignoring what that piñata has inside. Think of the stock market, playing lotto, betting on a horse race, and you see that the result is uncertain. Certainly, when the angels in my way decide for me, I think, they know what to choose because they know what my mission is. I have seen in the results of my stories a purpose that the angels follow to accomplish the tasks of my mission. I have learned that even when the result of an event does not help my interests still some of its circumstances maybe favorable to me. These circumstances may not be obvious, but if I seriously look for them, I find them. I understand that once an event concludes, we cannot change it; it becomes history in our memory. Life is a forward process with no turning back, and the circumstances and events can only delay its progress; we cannot do anything to change that. This fact tells me that in the bleak of situations, if I am alive, I may still do something to overcome these situations. Sometimes I do not even do anything because my angels do it for me. I tell in my stories of the benefits I received with my sufferings."

2 – Why My Mother Insisted on My Learning English

"Misti, can you tell us about your school experiences."

"It all started with my mother's wish that I attended a private religious school; a bilingual, English and Spanish, school. She was determined that I learned English in such school. I did not understand why my mother insisted on that I learned that language. Neither my mother nor my father knew English, nor had we been in an English-speaking country. We had no relatives who could speak English, and we had no acquaintances in those countries, why that much insistence? Why did she want me to learn English? My mother never explained to me the basis of her interest or her insistence. It was something that she did not know why either. I did not like that language, and I found out that, it was more difficult to speak it than understand it. I followed what she wanted me to do even though I disagreed with her decision. My mother could have not anticipated that United States would become a dominant power in the world at the end of the Second World War. Even if she could, how could that situation serve me? My parents and relatives did not talk about politics, although I learned much later that they talked about the war. That war changed the course of the world and I learned later that the United States became a world power. My mother did not like either local or foreign politics; she was a woman raised by old family traditions.

"My country was poor and small that it did not have the capacity of influencing those world changes. One thing I say with respect to English, I liked to browse fashion and clothing magazines that I found at my Aunt Yolanda's shop. She worked in dress confection and customized sawing to order. I liked to look at the pictures of the latest fashion and dress styles in America in those magazines. I had friends in school that often traveled to New York, Los Angeles, and Miami, and they told me about those cities; but I remember I had no interest or desire to visit those places. I pay little attention to what they said, or perhaps I occupied my thoughts on other issues. My school years in that catholic, bilingual school, went by fast; and although I learned some English to satisfy my mother, I believed it was little."

"Did you have many friends?"

"Yes, among my friends, there was Mitza, whom I considered another sister. Her parents were our neighbors. Their house was close to ours and in the same vicinity. I often spent the whole day in her house when I had no classes. Mitza's parents liked me much, and they were close friends of my parents. We strolled the outdoor, went to the beaches and to picnics at my grand parents' farm; we attended family occasions, sharing friendship. I grew together with Mitza, and I consider her my best friend. We must have a best friend, one that we may trust our private issues. She attended her first school grades in an American school, and I would have enjoyed attending that school with her. I always said to my mother, 'Mother, if you want me to learn English you should enroll me in that American school where Mitza goes?' My mother did not answer my question."

3 – *All situations are transitory.*

"Misti, do you wish to keep things or conditions forever?"

"No, not really, I have learned that situations and things are not permanent and change on a continuous basis in my life. Alina, Mitza's aunt, and her daughter had moved to America Martha in 1956; Mitza moved to live with them in 1960, at that time, I lost my best friend. Mitza's parents let her go to America to live with her aunt, and that surprised me because her parents did not let her go out of the house alone. I say that they worried much about the safety and well-being of their two daughters; they did not allow them to go out on their own to other people's houses. I do not understand why they allow her to go; as always, I say, for some unknown reason things occur and by walking along in life, I understand the reason in time. It always saddens me when I think that happy situations, moments, and good things end. These situations or things are not permanent.

"Mitza always wrote to me, and she told me in her letters about her life with her aunt in America. She always came on vacations. We spent time together talking about children's things, but we talked about life when we were much older. I told her about that rigid regime in my house. I talked with her about my mother's passionate insistence that I learned English well. Mitza asked me to go to America with her, adding that I would study and learn English better and faster there. I said, 'I do not know'. In my mind, the answer was easy, I could not decide for myself, and this situation urged me to think about what my mother might say if I asked her. It was my fear of being me making my own choices, making my own decisions, and it was true, I could not make that decision myself."

Chapter 4

Angels came during My Adolescence

1 – Can a Friendship be Unacceptable?

"Misti, you mentioned about Mitza, your best friends, did you have a boy friend?"

"Of course, I had one and only one, my husband. Let me tell you, the years went by, and my teenage arrived with the consequential interest in boys. I had controversies with my mother more than with my father because of that interest. During those days, a boy had to have permission from the parents to visit a girl. My parents had to know the boy beforehand to grant permission. They also liked a sufficiently long courtship to get to know the boy. During a courtship, the boy asked the parents' permission to get married; the parents announce the engagement and set the date of the marriage. My mother disliked that I had male friends at my age, and those who visited me, they did it for a few times, and never returned. My mother sat with us in the formal living room when a boy visited me. She did not let us alone even for a minute. My mother accompanied me every time I went to parties; and if I danced more than two dances with the same boy, my mother began signaling displeasure saying, *'dance with other boys. It is not appropriate to dance with the same young man, or what is going on with that boy? Let us go, we are going home now.'* My mother's attitude annoyed me a lot; I was doing nothing improper besides enjoying my time. She always had excuses for rejecting any friend of mine. I felt as living with no will of my own because always I depended on her orders, doing what she said, and I disliked her excessive control.

2 – How can a Friendship be Impossible?

"A family with five boys moved in the neighborhood one day. I did not pay attention to the presence of the new neighbors for a long time. By whim, I began a friendship with one of those five boys,

Roger, and without my mother knowledge; I saw him on several occasions. My mother got angry when she found out; and her scolding and reprimanding started with a scandal. My mother thought that boy was not for me, as usual. She did not know that I did not intend to carry anything serious with Roger, and I did not tell her. For me, he was a point with what I demonstrated my rebellion claiming my rights, I thought. It was an impossible friendship; my parents did not agree with and I intended to have nothing serious with Roger."

3 – The United States Land of Miracles

"I sense that you were frustrated living under your parents rules, am I correct? Did you ever think about running away?"

"Oh! No, we do not think about running away from home; our social etiquette allows no behavior as that in my country. Of course, I was frustrated and I wanted to change that condition, but I wanted not to upset my parents.

"Mitza came on vacations that year, and she again suggested that I should go to finish my studies in that country. I neither wanted nor desired to go away from my country, but she did not know that I had reasons to consider that. I knew that my parents would not approve my trip because they were conservative. My parents told me that I could go to America to finish my studies, a few days later. It was a complete surprise for me, and I thought about what could have made them accept my traveling. I learned later that Mitza's parents talked to my parents about this issue. Once again, I asked, 'why do I need to learn English? What do I gain by going to America? What is there for me?'

"Of course, I would finish learning English in the United States and my mother's insistence would realize. I had two years left to finish my high school, and my parents consent would be an opportunity for me to stay out of their control. My mother may satisfy her hope that I finish learning English; my parents were happy with the idea that I would stay away from Roger for while. Perhaps they thought that my relationship with Roger should end because it could end up in a disaster. My parents did not know that I indeed did not want anything serious with Roger. I used him as recourse to challenge my mother's authority. I accepted their proposal thinking that it would be for two years and maybe I would not miss much."

"Were you surprise of the outcome and the opportunity to come to USA?"

"I have no doubt that the angels had set the scenario; there were many issues and subjects needing to be coordinated at once. First, my mother had an adamant insistence that I learned English. Second, my parents did not accept my friendship with Roger. Third, Mitza's had suggested that I go to USA and finish my high school there. Fourth, Mitza's parents convinced my parents to let me go to America. It was a perfect plot where everything fitted well; all things happened that way for me. I thought that, for some reason, my mother insisted on my learning English and Roger appeared in my way. I think that the angels incited Mitza to say that I should finish my studies in America. I could not see the forces that pushed Mitza's parents to encourage my parents to let me go to USA; I never requested their assistance. I asked myself, 'why did my parents decide to let me go?' I never had lived alone, and my mother and my grandmother, Ivana, always took care of me. One more obstacle required attention; I needed protection and care while I stayed in America, 'who can provide that for me?' Mitza's aunt, Mrs. Alina, accepted me as a guest living in her house, and that solved that other obstacle. I saw how convenient it was to have Mrs. Alina in position to provide room and board. In summary, I thought that in this act they all conspired to make my trip to America possible. In fact, everybody acted on their own; they had no influence from each other but had a common goal, to facilitate my trip to USA. This event happened in a smooth and easy manner; I thought the angels manipulated subjects to act in a definite way. I wondered why they made everything easy for me. I wondered why they did not include me in the final decision affecting my life. It was obvious that I was the main character of this story. I felt as if, in fact, everyone wanted to transfer me to that country changing the course of my life, for a reason I ignored. I did not want to go. I put nothing of my part to materialize that trip, and I contributed the least in that choosing, but I went along with that decision anyway."

"Did you have a visa ready? How did you travel to USA? "

"No, I did not have a visa; my parents applied for my student visa for me at the US American Embassy in my country. They responded to us quickly, and we when we went to pick up my student visa a week later. For me, it was exceedingly fast; my friends had told me that the process could take three to four months. They offered a permanent residence for me, instead of the student visa we asked for. In this way, I could remain in America if I desired. I overcame my timidity and obedience, and asked my mother, 'if I liked that place, mom, may

I remain there?' She answered that she would think about it, but for the moment, I had to return when I had finished my studies. My mother revealed her intention with her response. My mother excluded from her plan the possibility for me to stay in that country more than the time for my studies. Her intention was unique for me; I would go to study there and return home when I completed my schooling. She excluded from her plan everything that was not my learning English and making my life in my country. That is the way it was, all easy, all simple, as if all the characters in this production rehearsed their role with care. I traveled to the United States because of this first mayor decision that changed the course of my young life. Perhaps, I will know the reason later on in my life, but I asked, 'what has this life for me? What has luck for me? Will this change help or hinder my life?' I would like to know, Heaven knows, what comes ahead. During the time of my long flight to America, my questions roar louder in my head than the twin-engine of the PANAM's airplane. I thought for a long time, but, finally, I said to myself, 'go to sleep; the answer to your questions will come with time.'"

"Wow, that plot was well executed, were you surprised?"

"Yes, it surprised me to see how fast and smooth all these events happened, and since that time, I thought, 'for what reason?'Ever since then, I have been studying the bases supporting each event in the evolution of my life. I need to know the reasons and intentions of those who get involved in my decision process; but I still need to understand the purpose of their involvement. 'What did anybody except me gain after all?' Those questions hovered in my mind until; at last, in the solitude of my room, I heard the messages and connections. I saw for the first time how the angels in my way integrated and completed the cast, this first act of their masterpiece, and the curtain came up. I saw the plot of this film; 'a teenage girl goes to the United States with a predefined intention, to study, graduate and return to her native origin with no delay upon finishing her school.' What was the purpose for that neat plot? I had no answer and I decided to study the angels' actions in detail."

"That sounds as a premier movie plan shown on a marquee, does it not?"

"I see that now that you mentioned it. I saw the reasons for which the circumstances carried me to the United States. My mother was my first angel, or the subject the angels used to prepare me for that trip changing the course of my life. My trip to USA satisfied my mother's purpose; I was going to that country to advance my knowledge of English. At the same time, I was going there to prepare myself to open doors of opportunities in front of me. I was going there to test my wings in my first solo flight. Maybe my mother was the voice, not an angel, through which my angels expressed their intention, through her mind; she was always consistent and adamant, restricting my opposition to learn that language. My angels provided a simple solution for my trip to America, because, I saw they knew that I would have to go there. They managed the circumstances of the events; and coordinated the sequence of actions of those involved in this story of my trip.

"The angels brought Roger to our neighborhood at a precise place and time; my friendship with him created that undesirable and risky situation with my parents. My mother, of course, objected my friendship with Roger; and my angels used him as a wild card to complete the conditions making up that trip. The angels also found and induced Mrs. Alina to offer board and room and protection for me. They knew that Mitza was living there with her aunt; thus, she became the perfect companion for me. These three conditions were essential for my trip to USA; otherwise, my parents would have rejected that idea. Besides, of all that, I had a desire to escape my family's restrictive environment; thus, I accepted the idea and my trip desire came true. That was my subtle escape to the United State. There was no doubt for me that the angels arranged the scenario and circumstances to make my traveling possible. For instance, I saw Mitza's insistence on that I finished my high school in America. It was also necessary that the school I was to attend was ready. The angels put together all these conditions to get the result. I could not have managed all these conditions alone to make my trip possible. The angels used years in managing and arranging the conditions for my trip. Now, the embroiderer of my life had its first act completed. As I walked in time, I discovered strange paths in my life. It may not be worth looking for the reasons of how the circumstances come together, but I am sure there can be many. I wanted to know the reason of my life because I love life; I consider that subjects or objects that have no meaning are not real or do not exist."

"Can you point out the guardian angels working in this episode?"

"In this story, I saw my angels in several essential forms. First, I saw my mother insisting for many years that I studied English. Second, I saw Mitza studying in USA and insisting that I finished my studies there. Third, I found Roger creating an undesirable friendship with me. Fourth, I get Mrs. Alina providing room and board for me in America. Fifth, I knew of Mitza's parents convincing my parents. Sixth, I included the US Immigration officer that gave me a permanent residence visa even though I did not know for what. Seventh, I thank my father for allowing my trip. All acted and contributed in order that this change in my life was possible. I failed to see why the immigration officer gave me a permanent residence at that time; I just needed a student visa. Will it bring any benefit to me? I do not know at this time, but it was clear, at the onset that I would return upon completing my studies. Nevertheless, I will wait to see when the permanent visa ties in with a future event."

"Why did you take a permanent resident visa? You knew that you were going to return to your country to live permanently."

"I did not really know why. For me, a permanent residence visa was an excess that would be lost when I returned to my native country. We accepted, however, a permanent visa without questions. Now, looking back from the reality of the whole map, I understand the strategy of the angels' plan that I follow. The angels found the obstacles that could have impeded my trip and worked with diligence and patience to neutralize them one by one. I needed to finish my education, including learning English; I had no knowledge of the purpose my mother had me to study English; I knew that studying English in my country was a futile endeavor. My parents would not let me go to a foreign country alone; they would require guaranteed safety for me. My parent had those reasons for not permitting my traveling. We still had to satisfy the requirements for my visa before I could plan my trip. There may be others obstacles that may escape my memory. This story let us see that the angels worked on my mother's head, and they revealed their work with her insistence that I learned that language. The angels found a secure place with Alina, who warranted care and safety for me. They found Mitza's friendship that was going to accompany me. The angels found in Roger another strong reason for my parents to decide on sending me abroad. The angels made the process of my visa easy and quick; they even granted me a permanent residence. They found one more obstacle, my school; but they found the school I would attend in America and made it ready to accept me upon arrival. They made a perfect plan for my trip to America; it was no dream of mine, but the circumstances the angels created. For me, it was like falling in a current with no strength to swim out. That current washed me away towards an end that I did not understand. I said,' that was my life and my destiny. 'That was how they made my trip a reality."

"That episode made sense and it appeared logical. Misty, have you studied this subject in detail? Was your life as student a challenge in America? Did you like that State where you lived?" Misti paused for a moment as if arranging her thoughts to respond properly.

"It just happened that way. I did not put much into the circumstances yielding that result; and yes, I have studied these experiences repeatedly. I always pondered about why things converge to one purpose, helping me. Why do they come as easy as they come; life is not that simple, is it?"

"No, it is not; I think."

Chapter 5

It is Nice to Live in USA

1 – Life as Student in America

"I came to America and met Mitza's aunt, Mrs. Alina. Immediately, I knew that I was falling again in the hands of someone who would decide my life for me. She had a harsh manner to go about her relations with others. She was rude speaking in an insensitive way that seemed offensive sometimes; however, she was protective and worked beyond her duty to protect and keep us safe. Mrs. Alina set clear rules of the game for me. These rules included my study first, no male friends, no dating or going out with friends, or parties that distracted my scholastic tasks. Nevertheless, I was content, and in a short time, I learned to do house cleaning, washing and ironing my clothes and cooking. Mrs. Alina thought I was a teenage girl who never had done house duties, and she was right because I had never done house duties before. Indeed, I was preparing to be on my own here, and once again, I confirmed that things occurred to support other things to occur later. I took that I was learning to take care of myself learning household duties, for a specific reason. I learned that people must be self-sufficient to take care of their own affairs in America. In my case, Mrs. Alina was responsible for my security, health, and care and I had to care for the rest of my personal needs.

"A new phase of my life began, and surprised and scared I thought about what purpose this would serve. I received funds from my parents to pay for my stay every month; I did not need anything else. I was happy with my friend, Mitza, and I was busy with my schoolwork. Mitza and I walked together to school; it was a short distance, and we enjoyed that path through the alleys bordered with tall eucalyptus trees, full of foliage. A chorus of birds sang celebrating the beginning of each new day. Those beautiful days, full of happiness and with no worries were only memories we kept now. I was happy enjoying Mitza's friendship and studying; and I was thankful of

Mrs. Alina's kindness. In the beginning, those rules were OK by me; however, after a while, my life was a routine empty of adventures proper of adolescents. I know it is nobody faults; I had accepted them. We had happy moments and laughers that broke that monotony, but my soul was lonely. We went to the movies, walked at parks, and went shopping to stores nearby and supermarkets always with Mrs. Alina. This implanted routine prevailed no matter what; however, I felt a high pressure, a sensation that this routine was about to crack. I ignored when or how, but I felt it was coming. My soul was lonely; I needed something to attached to."

2 – How I met My Enchanted Prince.

"What did you do for social relation in America, did you have any friends?"

"Not so much as I would like. I had several friends, and let me tell you about one in particular. It was early December; Mitza worked in a store chain, May Co, in the downtown of that city. I had come to that store to wait for Mitza at the end of her shift that day. I remember seeing Martha, Mrs. Alina's daughter, coming down an electric escalator; she said in a loud voice, 'a friend of mine is coming to pick us up. He is a friend of many years that I have not seen. He is coming in his car, and he will give us a ride home, let us wait for him at the corner'. That news did not have any significance for me other than a ride home, and besides, he came for Martha, not for me; however, Martha's emotions touched me somehow. I had never seen her thrilled as that; and we waited a long time for her friend.

"At last, Martha's friend arrived with another man, Rufino, Mrs. Alina's friend whom we knew because of her visits to the house. They came on foot because they had parked their car in a public parking nearby. Martha's friend introduced himself as Rangel, and while we all walked back to the parking lot, he told Martha; 'Misti is beautiful but young, I like her'. They continued talking in tight and fast English that I understood little of what they were saying. To me he looked sure of himself, rough and rude and at times thinking too high of himself. Rangel's demeanor was contrary to my social manners; since that moment, I despised him. Rangel had come out of the army, and by coincidence, his friend Rufino had brought him to Mrs. Alina. Rangel had not seen Mrs. Alina and Martha for several years; he stopped seeing them several years ago. Later, I knew that it was not

Rangel desire to visit Martha's mother that afternoon. It was because of Rufino dirty scheme to bring him to Mrs. Alina's house. After all, that was not my business, and I did not care. I was a guest in Mitza's aunt house, and thus I did not have a say on that. From that day on, Rangel visited the house. I socialized with Rangel in family gatherings, by courtesy; but always told Mitza how I felt about him, 'I cannot stand him. He thinks too much of himself'. Nevertheless, Rangel showed an interest in me, and I knew later that I was the reason of his visits. Rangel was intelligent and had some tender, sentimental, romantic sides that I cannot deny; I need to be fair and just. The days went by, and Rangel gain my trust, little by little, and my sentiments to the point that I accepted him as he was. I was sad and lonely in that environment when Rangel came into my life; this was the important event of this relationship, he came when I needed company. I knew that once Mitza finished her high school she would return to that native country. I also had the same destiny because I had promised my parents I would go back when I finished my studies. That feeling and my commitment blocked my desire of tying me to this environment or to any person.

"I tell these stories thinking that I am not the center of everything; I would portray an egotistical image of me I do not wish. I must say that I receive the greater benefits from the results of circumstances and events. Why did Rangel come to Mrs. Alina's house that afternoon in December? If it had not been for Rufino's dirty scheme, Rangel had not comeback to Mrs. Alina's house. Let us see; neither Mrs. Alina nor Mitza drew any benefit off Rangel comeback, outside of the joy of seeing him again. I learned later that he was coming to see me, not Mrs. Alina or Mitza. Rangel filled my loneliness and helped me with my schoolwork. He said he would finish his career because he was out of the service; he had completed two years of engineering before the Army drafted him. I attached to his qualities, little by little; however, I could neither lean much on false hopes nor take in a serious relationship. I knew that I had to leave him when I return to my native country at the end. That was a feeling of uncertainty and deep grief. Rufino and Martha's helped me to see Rangel; that was the only way I could possibly meet him. It seemed that they were in charge of caring that my friendship with Rangel was not lost. Mrs. Alina's did not know of my meeting Rangel. I knew well that she would not approve anything else beyond Rangel's friendship with the family. I felt guilty of breaking the rules Mrs. Alina set upon my arrival. I thought 'that was life'. I remembered the situation I went through with my parents because of my friendship with Roger. I know that history does not repeat itself. All current circumstances, events, and results are new; they may look similar to concluded ones, but they are different. Life is forward moving and does not go back to rewrite concluded events. I respect the commitment I made to my parents, so I cannot act freely to follow my sentiments. I felt that I continued subjected to the will and rules of others as Mrs. Alina established rules of the game. I was sure of Rangel's arrival to Mrs. Alinas's house was casual and without his wanting. Rangel arrived in time for me to know him and to consider him as my companion while I stayed without my friend Mitza in this country. It was a time, just and necessary, to found out if Rangel may be my enchanted prince in my life story. I think that the angels come as part of a premeditated larger plan of actions, not by mere casualty. I have seen their premeditated actions in the precise timing with which things and beings appeared and in the results of an event. I know we are not able to change with certainty all of the circumstances of any event to get a desired result. I know that it is arrogant and egoist to think that the world spins about my individual existence. I prefer to believe that angels in my way keep me satisfied for a mission that I did not yet understand, but I could not fail. It may be better for me to accept this than to think that all is a matter of fate. I sadden thinking that I live for a mission and not for my own self because it is like being a pawn in the chess game of my life."

3 – Life in Solitude with My Angels

"Did you have to return to your native country, Misti? Why can you stay and further your education?"

"You know, Miguel, I did think of that; however, my ethical philosophy is that I must honor my commitments. I agreed with my parents that I would go back after I finish my high school work.

"Mitza finished her school in Jun of 1965, and the day to return to her parents' house came with her graduation. The happy days with Mitza ended; I felt sad seeing that this enchanting time was transitory. It was an extended moment and as moment must end. I thought of Rangel also because my relation with him had its time and its end. It was not within my power to change Mitza and Rangel paths, and I had to take the evolving results with resignation. What an irony this is because even the circumstances did not allow me to make my own choices. 'Can you tell me why?' I know what I wanted, but I could not choose that because the circumstances did not let me. It was as if they gave me something for a moment, and tool it away from me later. What was the purpose of my life, if I could not choose? Tell me, what was it? That was why I could neither give in nor attach myself to anything or anybody; because, I knew that, those situations might not be there the next day. I felt that I had a half-life; what I wanted to do is not what I had to do. In fact, I could not disclose my yearning and the fact that Rangel had kept me company and gave his understanding during my stay in USA. I thought my angels used Rangel as a subject to accompany me for the short time I was alone in this great country. I thought this other angel appeared in my way for that reason. I never thought of staying in this country even though I liked this city since I came."

"What did you like about this country that could have made you stay?"

"For me, this was a place where the individual is free to act and do what the individual wants. It pleased me much to see the safety that existed during those days. Merchants used to let the milk, the bread, and the newspaper at the front door, including the bill, the payment in cash, and the change. What attracted me was the respect the citizens gave each other; it also impressed me to see how neighbors did not involve in each other's businesses. I saw how the people enjoyed their freedom living in peace and managing their own business.

"Mitza left, and I remained alone with Mrs. Alina. My life was not the same now; I returned from school to a house filled with silence every afternoon. Rangel came, and waited for me at the end of my classes sometimes, and we walked together through the alleys I used to walk with Mitza. He escorted and left me at home. Mrs. Alina did not like my friendship with Rangel and started to make my life impossible. On the contrary, Martha was sympathetic with my friendship with Rangel and eased my friendship with him. Martha was married and had three little boys that I baby-sat in her house sometimes. I thought it was best to break up with Rangel on several occasions, because I did not want to fail my promise to my parents; Mrs. Alina threatened me with writing to my parents saying that my friendship with Rangel did not let me study; but I could not break up with him. I realized that are always opposite forces fighting for a cause. Sometimes, both forces may have valid reasons, as in Mrs. Alina's case whose intention was to protect me, and my reason was to live my own life. Be it as it may;

those forces diverged, and in the end, the one closer to the truth prevailed to support my mission. I may not have been an honor student, but it was not true that I did not study; I studied in my way and at my pace until the end of my studies in 1966, when I graduated.

"The time was going by fast, and the last two semesters of my schooling came to end at last. Those were sad days pivoting and changing the course of my life again; I did not know where this change was taking me. I felt like walking blindfolded in a jungle where the circumstances were the trees. How could I have had confidence in the steps I took in that jungle? How could I know the trail I followed was the right one? How could I know if I took the correct choices? I thought that following the angels' guidance, and messages was, indeed, a safer way to go through life. The angels knew my mission, and they did what was best for me to accomplish that assignment."

"Did you sin in your actions by not going by Mrs. Alina rules?"

"No, I did not think so; I thought that Mrs. Alina's rules invaded my rights; I did not consider a sin to have friends, male or female. Let me say this about sinning, people think there is a sins-purging place, a waiting lobby after death, where sinners pay their sins with penitence; I think that sin-purging place is this world. Here, we walk without knowing our course and unable to avoid bumping against obstacles we find in the path. How can one be guilty of the choices and mistakes one makes, acting with no knowledge of the future? In other words, we choose not knowing all the circumstances around each choice ignoring the results of choice; in fact, we will never have absolute knowledge of the circumstances affecting an event. I know now that the angels come for this reason; I think that they are always present following God's orders to guide me in my walk through this jungle of circumstances. I have experienced that at the end of bleak situations something beneficial comes my way; thus, I feel secured and protected because of their presence, and I think it is reasonable for us to believe that.

"At the end of my studies, I went with Rangel to my graduation party. It was a farewell party, my last escapade; but I did not say anything. I knew I had to go home in June destined to live away from Rangel in my native country. I had an uncertain and heavy feeling that my relationship with Rangel would end; but I did not say anything. I had made a commitment to return home at the end of my studies, and that commitment was stronger than my feelings; but I said nothing to Rangel. My situation has proved to me that someone or the circumstances managed my life. I wanted to tell to the world of my situation; I wanted to tell of my inability to take what I wanted, and I had to quench my desires with silence. I did not say anything.

"I went back to my native country resigned to live there forever; I saw no possibility to go out of that country again. Rangel traveled with me in my mind and with him that sentimental love that had grown in my soul; those beautiful days remained floating as memories in my mind. Mitza was waiting for my return to continue our friendships and adventures together. She had been a terrific, supportive friend, advising and caring for me; and I also served as her companion; we helped each other mutually. Some days we think that life will end in boredom. Some hours we succumb distressed; but then we see the hand of angels offering to pick us up. We feel then secured comforted. This is the story of my life, the real experiences in journey of my mission."

Chapter 6

Living in My Native Country

1 – How I got My First Job in My Native Country

"What did you plan to do in your native country, did you think about that?"

"My plan was to find a job and to help my parents somehow, and I thought that getting a job could take a long time. I had not even started looking for a job; however, when one day Melba, a family friend, came to visit us. She said she worked for a car sales agency in the city down town; they were looking for an executive bilingual secretary for the Director. I could not hide my interest in that issue, and I asked her about the job requirements. She said she would investigate and arrange an interview for me. I went to that interview, and without problems, the Director gave me the job to start the next day. I felt that my angels used Melba as an instrument to expedite the event, getting a job. That job matched my knowledge and background; I thought they had designed that job for me.

"I went to work on the first day, and seating at the desk, I reflected on the way this job came to me. Between sighs and tears, I thought that my mother insistence on my learning English had a purpose; I had here a good justification of her insistence. Were the angels who seeded insistence in my mother's mind? I cannot say with precision what it was; however, reviewing the sequence of events, I knew that Melba had not visited my family for a long time. That day she came as a surprise to the family. For me, the purpose of her visit was to let me know about that job opening at her work place. Our conversation was about what she did, what her company did, and about the open position during her visit; it was as if she were trying to convince me to take that job.

"For me, all that effort and the trip to North America to complete my studies now revealed an aspect of its purpose. Getting a job here in my country was that easy and that fast, and I started to work. The days, endless days, were going by, and living with my parents, was monotonous. I did not need money because I did not go out much; in fact, I gave my mother all my wages taking something for my immediate, personal needs. For me, something was missing, anguish I did not understand. It seemed that a continuous calm stage came, but it was not true because within me, deep inside, I had no peace. I had an agony, an anxiety, longing for all that I had left in USA. I still had fresh in my mind the memories of what I left in America; but the thought that Rangel could forget me was even more painful and difficult."

"Did you miss your boyfriend much?

"Yes, I miss him; I cannot forget him. Rangel's letters came always sweet, romantic, and amorous; he told me all he was doing there and how much he missed me. The contrast between Rangel's world and mine highlighted the pain of a possible unwanted end; were there hopes for me? He was far from me, and I was here creating unsuccessful outcomes of our relationship. I was not negative, but I thought I had to stay in my country forever working to help my parents. It seemed at least that way to me. Roger did not figure in my way; I had no reason either to bring that episode of my capricious adolescence back. I went out with my friend, Mitza, to parties, hiking, alone with no dates and everything seemed empty. Rangel's letters always came to my house, and my parents always gave them to me when I came home from work in the afternoons. Those letters were a light at the end of my long, long, a dark tunnel longer than the time of my whole life. His letters were the medicament for my loneliness. At least that was what I felt and what saddened me."

2 – How Angels Managed My Marriage

"Did you think of marrying Rangel someday?"

"Of course, that was a possibility, even though it was remote. This story started on a day of November of 1966; that day my parents opened the last letter that Rangel sent me; they had no acceptable reason. I had not challenged my parents for anything before. They invaded my privacy and my property; it was something I could not believe they could do. I was furious and I protested their abuse this time; I told them,' that letter was mine, and you should not have opened my mail.' In that letter, Rangel asked me to marry him during his trip to see me in December; He said that only he would make that trip if I agreed to marry him. It was a serious situation for me, and I did not know what to do. My parents knew Rangel's proposal and made a scandal. I had to ask my parents' consent to marry Rangel, and had to obey my parents' decision. I would lose Rangel if they did not approve it. I always believed that relation with him was chimerical and that, in the end, the distance itself would diffuse it as smoke dispersed in the wind. Rangel had proposed in that letter to write my parents asking for my hand in marriage; however, he needed not to write because my parents knew of his intention. I thought their reaction would force the end of my story, of my relation with Rangel. The situation with my parents disturbed me; at the same time, I was encouraged by the emotion caused by Rangel's surprise. I decided that I would talk with my parents and would give him, an answer, yes or no. It was a life or death situation for me. That night, at bedtime, I let my grandma know the reasons for my wanting to marry Rangel. She advised to follow my heart on my decision. Her words encouraged me, and I planned to talk to my parents as soon as possible; however, it was unnecessary for me to initiate that climax. A few days later, while I was with my family at my uncle Mino's farm my father called me apart a few steps away from the family gathering. I was afraid of knowing what my father could tell me. I was afraid that my parents would kill my hope in its infancy, and I reluctantly walked those steps with him away from the group and waited. He told me the same thing that my grandma told me, 'My daughter, I want to say that I bless your marriage if your heart is ready for it'. My heart jumped off my chest because I expected a different response from my father. I felt my body trembling with emotion. Perhaps my tears looked out on my pupils, and I held back my feelings of surprise and relief, hiding behind my sobbing, my possible crying. It was an emotional moment for me. I did not know if I cry, laugh, or scream my feelings out, my sense of victory. I embraced my father with all the strength I had left in me, and I said, 'thanks dad a thousand times thanks'. My father loved me much, and I knew what my decision meant for him. For me, it was an emotional surprise filled with happiness, and at last, I had an instance in which I might make my choice on my own. I was making a decision that would change the course of my whole life permanently. I feared, yes feared, because those thoughts and feelings of receiving something that they would later take away from me came back to me again. I tamed my apprehensions and amid my doubts and emotions, I took the road opening for my life; my father's decision came in time.

"I was worried because my mother was managing my affairs once again; I knew that the environment was the same as when I left for America. That was why their decision was a surprise. I stretched my arms up to the sky and said, 'Wow, my parents accepted my marriage with Rangel setting the day for the end of this same year'. I could not believe it.

"Misty, what could have happened if your parents had said no?"

"I did not know, but that outcome could not have arrived at a more exacting time. Here, in this city nothing was as when I went to America two years before. The time that I spent in USA, as short as it was, was sufficient for the friends I had before I left to change their interests, their activities, and their routines. When I came back from America, I no longer had things or stories in common with them. They had continued their life in a scenario to which I no longer belonged. Those common roads we had in those days were separate and different after I returned to this city. My life was running in parallel with theirs, and had no point where they can come together again. Rangel's proposal came at the right time to give my parents time to think and accept my wedding, to allow time for the wedding activities; Rangel had only 25 days."

3 – How I Returned to Live in the United States

"Did you marry Rangel? Did you go back to USA?"

"Rangel came in at the beginning of December; we got married on the last day of that year 1966, and we flew back to the United States that same day. The course of my life was once again changed, and with this change, new question, new choices, and new decisions came. Now I was not alone anymore because my angel, Rangel, walked with me on a permanent basis. What happened with that letter out of my control was the key, an opening, to the impasse that had built up in my life path. That letter was the climax of the story of my marriage. I still wonder about what made my parents open that letter from Rangel; I thought it was too much of a coincidence that they picked up the letter wherein he asked me to marry him, and after the fact, I am glad they did.

"Did you ever think of going back to America to live there?"

"I never thought that I could return to the United States after I had come back to my country at the end of my studies. I neither looked for nor wanted to go to the United States; but there was something or someone pushing me towards that country. What else is there besides studying that language that I do not know well? My mother insisted on my learning English in those early school days, and she allowed my short trip to USA; but now after my marriage, it was definite that I was going back to this country permanently. I think that this event could not be a casuality of life; it was clear that it had a defined purpose. Could it be perhaps that Rangel was then, and he still is, indeed an instrument, another form, which my angels used so I could fulfill the mission of my life? I understood why the angels had brought Rangel into my way while in USA. They managed the time and circumstances so I could marry him and travel back to America. I had no doubts that my fate was to live in America; Rangel did not know; he was unaware that my angels had fixed the situation. The angels do not explain their acts; they make the events look natural and seamless happening in a subtle manner; however, they warn or announce us of their intention. In fact, if we observe the circumstances around us we may see that the events point out to an expected outcome. I saw their purpose of taking me to USA to study. I came to finish my high school and to setup the strings and conditions for future the circumstances and ties of coming events; events that would bring me back to USA. That was the reason why they placed Rangel in my way. 'Why did I fell in love with him even though that at the beginning I despised him?' For me it was obvious, the angels could not produce a stronger force for me to leave my parents, my family and my country, the force of love.

"I pondered for days and days about why my father changed his mind and consented my wedding. I did not find a logical reason that was compatible with their way of thinking. Why my father did changed his mind and allowed me to make a choice or decision that would change the course of my life? This change was forever beyond the point of return. That was something that perhaps I will never know the truth."

"Did you ever think about making such serious decision?"

"No; I never thought that I would have to make such serious decision. These thoughts never cross my mind before. In fact, I wrapped up myself in the drama of my marriage that I did not think about anything else; I did not think about leaving behind my parents, my relatives, and my family. We could not waste any time; we had no slack time available in the wedding activities and marriage process. We had to make exact and quick decisions for it to happen. I am sure that the angels incited my parents to open Rangel's letter. Their action set off the chain of events of my marriage that would have taken more time otherwise, but why did they do that? My parents did not decide against their social precepts or out their policies, but they did this time to my surprise. I think that the angels induced my parents to accept my marriage.

"I always asked myself; 'how could I leave my parents alone? What was the real mission they assigned me?' I always concluded the same; I will know later on. I thought that this was an act of my angels opening my parents' understanding to place my happiness ahead of their own lives. I realized at that time how fundamental it was to have gone to study in America. It was a necessary requirement for me to live in that country; and I was going back to it. The angels knew that I required certain conditions and means to live there in America; and the angels revealed those conditions and supports with their subtle actions. I saw the angels that acted in this episode. First, I found Rangel as my fiancé asking me in marriage. Second, I found my father in the second lead role. He discovered Rangel's plan to ask my father for my hand. My father denied that idea; however, in the end, he consented my wedding. Third, I cast the church clerk in a supporting role. He made our wedding application easy and smooth. Fourth, I cast the chief of immigration in a supporting role. He offered and gave me a permanent resident visa; and I understood the reason why. The purpose of that visa was clear and it was included in the embroidering of my life. That visa gave me the privilege to enter the United States with at any time.

"It would have been impossible for me to get a permanent residence visa in the short time Rangel had. He came, we got married, and he took me back to America in that short time; it was impossible otherwise. We had only one sequence of activities that we had to follow to go back to USA. That sequence was critical and unique path; each activity had just the time for completing. Each activity had no slack time for any other sequence outside of it. We could have not married if we had an error or delay on any of the activities in this critical path.

4 – My Reflections on how My Marriage happened

"Perhaps I can answer your last question; that is, 'If my parents had said no to my marriage. Let me say that there were several possibilities before we got to that point. If Rangel had forgotten me during the time I was away from him, what would I have done? Rangel could have given up our relationship and never ask me to marry him. In this case, everything would have ended, and I would have stayed in my country. The chance that Rangel could have come and my parents could have not allowed my marriage was also possible. What would have happened if my parents had maintained their negative position? In this case, again, everything would have ended and I would have remained in that country. What would have happened if the priests had rejected my wedding application? The church had not permitted my marriage, and the result would have been the same as the previous cases. Rangel had come; my parents had allowed our marriage but Rangel had lived in USA for a long time and had brought no proof of being single in that country. What would have happened if there had been no witnesses who testify that Rangel was single? There would not have been a marriage and the results would have been as before. If I had not married Rangel, what would I have done? I do not know the answers to these questions, excepting that the common result of all these situations was that I had to stay in my native country. It was a complex fault tree; my path had many branches or possibilities, but only one viable for me. It would have been my end if I had not married Rangel; I did no longer belong to that environment in which I had lost my old friends or had no common adventures with them, only memories. I was a stranger in my backyard there, and I had nothing left there excepting starting new relations with new friends. I think that my angels managed the circumstances and created a scenario that left no other choice for us. Once again, I felt that all the characters had conspired in making that new event a reality. The angels resolved the obstacles one by one until they got the result desired my wedding. I might have been wrong, and time would show if I am correct."

"What can you tell us about the result that came out?"

"I have said that my marriage happened quickly and smoothly; although, my parents had added suspense to that situation. In the end, my marriage was another decision made for a crucial change in life. The threads weaved and tied with this event advanced the picture on the embroiderer of my life. I had completed a significant part of my life. Now, I was alone with my husband, and out of my parents' control. It was a big step, an act of independence, my independence.

"I have seen the angels in action while making that event possible. It was a straightforward play run; but I did not participate in the decisions. 'Did you notice that in this story, Miguel?' I asked, 'I was going to live in America, did I have to? Why did I leave my parents and my family behind'? I said at that time, 'The answers to these questions are in the future, and I will look for the reasons they had to make that result possible'."

Chapter 7

Return to USA after Marriage

1 – My Married Life Back in USA

"What were your plans once you got back to USA?"

"Rangel's life and mine had merged for the rest of the days we have left. As he said, we determined that this union is until death separates us. Since that day, we walked on the same trail and although, our angels may be different they have a common purpose now. I think there must be a reason for wedding Rangel, and it was the last requirement to fix my life in America; this gave me a reliable support and security. 'What is next?' I asked. 'What purpose is there for me?' These questions will remain in my mind until I find their answer with time. Meanwhile, I was happy alone with Rangel. I had a different life, a free life. We went out wherever we wanted and did what we wished together.

"Who do you think is the number one angel in this episode?"

"I do not forget Mitza. Because of her, I came to USA to study. Because I came to America, I met Rangel. Because I met Rangel I married him, and I returned to USA. She married and returned to America as if her destiny were to live in this country. Her support with respect to my mission concluded in the weaving of the embroiderer of my life. Now, we have a close friendship remaining through the distance. I would be arrogant if I thought that everything orbited around my life and for me alone. That is ironic because it is untrue. In this existence, each one goes on one's way following a set course towards the lighthouse marking the end of one's mission. I think that it is our duty in life side stepping to help others in their endeavors, continuing our way after that action. We should not anchor our life to friendships or temporary conditions no matter how appealing these may seem to us; friendships and conditions are transient most of the time. That was the case with Rangel and me before the wedding. I faced the chance that my relationship with Rangel could have died at the onset. That was the case with the scenario of my native country; when I came back, it was no longer my environment. I believe the angels in my way worked to change that. They used strings, ties, or threads and created links waiting for future mooring in the embroiderer of my life. Mitza will always be my friend across the distance; we live 3500 miles away apart. I will always thank her for what she did in getting me out of my country's scenario; I consider it was a crucial pivotal event in my life. Now, we walk on parallel paths as railroad tracks that never come together in the way. Indeed, we do not know our future. That is right, nobody can predict the future because it is always waiting for an event to occur; and when that event happens, it scoots over ahead to wait for another one. I do not know if I will ever serve as angel's instrument in any situation that may change the course of her life. If that need comes, I will be ready to collaborate with her goals as she collaborated with me. Having said that, I think, however, Rangel is the lead angel in this episode."

"Tell me about your experiences with the angels during your married life."

"Maybe saying that my wedding was small and private is embarrassing, but for me, it was incredible. The joy I felt that day made me feel so happy that my chest was too small to hold all my happiness. My marriage was a breakthrough result in the weaving of the embroidering of my life; it fixed the moorings, connections and ties forever on this part of the picture of the journey I follow.

"Although Rangel had his work waiting for him, our beginning was almost from zero. We came to live in a furnished apartment few blocks away from his work for many months. All was well with us while we adjusted to our means and married life environment, as fast as we could. I was adapting to that city and learning to act on my own, caring for my husband, the apartment, and myself. We decided to have no children allowing time to plan and adapt to each other for a couple of years. One day, Rangel closed his business and he went on to finish his engineering career. He got a job and while he worked in engineering design, he studied for his degree. I stayed alone in our apartment while he was at work during the day or went to the university at night. I wanted to have something on which I could occupy my mind and energy. I needed something that set objectives to my mind, a job."

2 – How I got My First Job in America

"Did you go to work after you came back to USA?"

"Not right away, although it was something I wanted to do. My husband understood me and agreed that I looked for a job; however, without previous work history or a resume that included more than my high school; the possibilities were few and that scared me. Few days went by before Rangel found an employment agency nearby. He took me there to fill out the agency application and to interview with an agent. The agent understood my lack of experience; but he composed a resume based on my studies and the work experience I had in my native country; and he sent me to an underwriting company for an interview. I was so scared that I could not speak my English well, stuttering when I interviewed with Mr. Jones, the manager, that morning. Mr. Jones understood my limited skills; however, he said I could have the job if the supervisor and I could understand each other. I walk out of Mr. Jones's office shocked by his decision; and I thanked him and my angels in between my sobs of gratefulness. While I waited for the Supervisor, I thought about how this person may see my second interview; after all, the supervisor would decide if I get the job.

"Finally, the supervisor, Margot, came and led me to her office; at the end of that interview, she decided she could work with me. The job was mine; I had to manage the company's document flow and distribution. Amid my overwhelming happiness, I saw how the angels solved my work yearning; but brought more questions to me. I did not believe that they had no better-qualified person than I in their list of candidates. Why this interviewing process was so easy and quick? It did not seem normal. Why were they replacing a capable person who had many years of experience with me? I was a beginner with no experience. Thus, it was. My decision to work was another action that changed the course of my life giving me the freedom of self-expression I looked for. Why did they give me that job? I did not know; I knew that my background and experience did not match the original requirements of that position at that time. I think my angels found and accommodated the players and circumstances helping me to get my first job. I saw the angels' plan of actions and their strategy with all the objects and subjects they used to solve the obstacles for me to get that job. In that case, I listed those elements as follows. I needed to have a resume that match the requirements of that position. I had to be able to please the supervisor with my spoken English. I needed to have acceptable aptitude to learn the work procedures in a short time. Reviewing the details, I found, three key elements for which I missed qualifying; however, my angels solved those obstacles one by one. The employment agent wrote my resume; Mr. Jones waved the skill requirements; and the supervisor accepted my English skills and decided to dedicate some of her time to train me well. I put nothing more than my interest and desire to work in this decision; the characters involved in this act did the rest. The angels handed the risk over to the manager and the supervisor who gave me that job. The angels knew what was coming; thus, they managed the circumstances, objects, and subjects before I went to that agency to precipitate the conditions I needed to get my job. It was obvious that I could have not done all that by myself. I did not know the circumstances or the requirements for this event to happen."

"It seems that you have experience reviewing each episode, Misty, how do you do it?"

"It is obvious that we do not manage the major events of our lives. I know that all events are circumstantial; and the circumstances or conditions shape the events. An event happens only when it meets the conditions and circumstances that form it; and the event yields its result. The point is that if we want to get a definite result, we would need to manage those circumstances and conditions that form this event. This is why I say that the angels intervened in the process of getting those definite results. An event requires a scenario, certain ground rules, the rules of the event, and the players; and all these are the conditions, circumstances, and the characters to perform the event. I had indentified the scenario for my job quest at the onset. I saw three main stages in this story; these are my house, an employment agency, and an underwriters company. I saw the procedures and the sequence of activities in each event; and I followed the circumstances of the events that the angels included in their plot. This plot included the conditions, the circumstances, and my desire to work. For me, it was easy to spot the characters and stage setting required for an act; and I found the angels in this event. My husband who decided to let me work. His role was that of facilitator and mentor. Mr. Jones, who reduced the requirements of that position; and the supervisor, Margot, who decided she could work with me. The placement agent was the fourth main character in this story; but that was not all. Getting that job was not simple, even though everything was easy and smooth.

"I saw that the angels had to prepare and solve several obstacles as fast as possible. I say that the angel many waved things otherwise required in order for me to take that position; the process did not seem normal to me. I asked myself, is that a preferential treatment for what reason, why for me. Why do I receive that much attention? I understood that I am part of a higher purpose that the angels follow to guiding my actions; but it was not because I had privileges others do not have. That would be unfair and unbecoming in the Kingdom of God. If we have a mission in our short lives, we must perform the actions that helps accomplish that mission quickly and exactly.

"I learned I had a mission to accomplish; and the angels came to help me guiding my actions and facilitating my well-being. I had to fulfill this objective to prepare for the next steps along my way, and Rangel played a decisive role. When I meditated on that issue, I saw my ignorance of the future and it made me feel afraid. I knew at that time, I had a mission; 'but what is the mission they had assigned me?'I did not know. 'What was Rangel's role in my life?'I did not know either. I have seen how the angels use their instruments; I have seen how they later separate the circumstances, objects, and subjects of an event. I confirmed my thoughts about wanting to be the one who makes my choices and decisions; I am not in control. In reviewing the details of the circumstances of my first employment, I saw that I did little to obtain that position, except contributing with my presence. Someone could say, 'you underestimated yourself;' but in fact, I, and only I, knew what I could or could not contribute to that event. Getting that job was as winning a lottery when there is a low probability of receiving the prize, but I got it. Why do they make it easy for me? I do not really know; I think there is a bigger plan, and I have a part in it. I believe that each one of us is part of a bigger plan and have a mission in life.

"Whenever I thought about my angels, I confirmed they did not appear in the common form people believe. They appear in many forms as in the case of my first employment. They used people to carry actions that helped me to get that job; and the result advanced the weaving of the embroidering of my life. I did not know what made the people decide as they did; however, I believed they did not have a choice because they were reacting to thoughts they follow, and perhaps they were not aware how these came to their heads. I received the benefit for the risk they took as we have seen. The manager told me what he expected of a candidate for that job, at the start of our interview; I saw that my qualifications did not meet his expectation.

I thought the manager could not have seen my ability to handle the job just from my responses during that interview; however, they gave me the job.

"Yes, someone could have said that it was a pure stroke of luck, and it might have been; but in my case, my strokes of luck are frequent and specific. I think that people have had similar cases with noticeable frequency, but they might have failed to observe them most of the time. On the one hand, I see that something that happens in my way serves as a base for which it follows ahead in life; and in the other hand, I think that we have to be susceptible and attentive to catch subtleties of the origin of events."

"How do you relate these events to the embroiderer of your life?"

"I had not seen clearly yet the bases and subtleties of the weaving of the embroiderer of my life. However, I have seen that each past event linked or moored with an occurring event advancing the weaving of that embroidering. Those links functioned as stretched little arms with opened hands waiting to clasp a little hand that appears in the future to make a connection. It is curious of course, to note that it is not any little hand that appears. This is not a random process; it has a definite purpose. Each little hand must meet the requirements of its matching hand. These links make a flawless weaving and keeps the quality of the embroidering of one's life. Thus, many connections of hands or many thread moorings made the nodes or knots of the embroidering of my life. Do not ask me when that embroidering will end because I would not know what to respond. Nobody can see the future, but I am sure of one thing, something that happened now serves as the base for another that will happen ahead. Thus, we should observe the weaving of our own embroidering, paying attention to the details of the picture that forms on them; we may then begin to see our mission in life."

3 – How my Family Grew

"I understand you delayed having your children. How did you family grow?"

"My first son, Keith, was born almost two years after we married, and I left my job just before his birth to start caring for him besides my husband and the apartment. I was doing well in my job and my work performance was excellent; I pleased the manager and the supervisor exceeding their expectations. He offered to keep my job in case I wanted to return after I had my son. My husband changed his career and was doing well. We had moved to another apartment and the owners hired us to manage their apartment building. I saw that my decision to work was positive. I knew that I could go back to work whenever I wanted.

4 – Dora, my New Friend

"One day I found out that a couple, Dora and her husband Daniel and his son, Daniel Jr., lived in one of the apartments in one of the buildings we managed. They were from my native country. When Rangel also went to his work, I stayed alone with my son in my office-apartment all the day. Dora also stayed alone with her boy for a similar reason. We kept company to each other until Rangel and Daniel returned from their work in the afternoons. We began a convenient friendship for both of us at the beginning; and it turned into a long lasting friendship. I sympathized with Dora since I met her, feeling as if I knew her for a long time ago. My thoughts flew fast to the threads of the embroidering of my life. What role would the new beginning relationship played in my life? In short, I knew that the opportunity to identify a reason comes with time; however, I could not stop thinking about the role of this new friend.

"I did not have to wait long before the situation gave me the answer I was waiting for. I had my second son, Kristian, almost a year after Keith birth, and my daughter, Marla, came about two years later; Dora expected her daughter, Laura, about the same day. She played an important role during that time providing the help I needed while I cared for my children. The next day after my daughter's birth, my husband and my children traveled to visit my parents. Dora offered me her help while I was alone with my daughter until my husband's return. My children remained with their grandparents that summer and returned in August. Dora always helped me since she did not have to go to work. I thought, 'friends are not for the help we receive from them; friend are for the sharing of the feelings they have for each other."

"Several months had passed by since my daughter birth, and I had no greater events during that time. I continued taking care of my children and my house. Rangel had found a job and was working in engineering. He had gone ahead with his studies to get his master degree in engineering. Our family had grown and doing well; we did not need much more. I felt settled; we had a solid basic life with no critical needs or urges. The angels had kept us fulfilled."

5 – *Abrupt Return to My Native Land*

"Why did you go back to your native country?"

"We felt nostalgia of our native country. While my husband finished his master's degree, we worked on a plan to return to our native country. Apprehensions and fears filled my head, and I began to study our urgency. 'Was this urge to return real? Did it have a meaning?'I did not think so; Rangel had gained a leading position in research and development with a high salary. He had a plan to go on to get a doctorate degree in environmental systems. Besides, we had nothing waiting for us in our native country. Rangel did not even have a job prospect. Our idea of returning to our native country was more than foolish; it was ridiculous."

"Misti, you said your country was an empty scenario and loaded with uncertainties and risks; and you said that your family situation was fine; why did you go back to your country?"

"We were blind and we knew it; however, even knowing that, we hurried into that risk. We both analyzed the conditions many times, but we were unable to change that idea. It was as if we were hypnotized and we had no control over our thoughts. In fact, our illusion was stronger than the reality we faced. We looked for reasons that justified the joint decision to go; we did not endeavor on finding reasons for not going. We came out with many excuses. We said, 'our children will meet and live with their grandparents and relatives'; we said, 'our children will learn a new language and lifestyle'. We compared the reasons of our intention. We analyzed the risks and the benefits of our decision; however, the results did not favor us. I questioned, why did we have to return when everything was going well for us? We had no reason to go, but we went, leaving behind a success that we had already obtained. It was crazy. I did not understand why. I thought that my angels created our unbreakable urge to return to our native country for reason I did not know."

"Misti, it was crazy indeed and risky, can you explain that?"

"Unknown forces behind our preposterous action rang in the bell tower of my mind incessantly; but I could not find the celebration for which they rang. I could find no reason for such urgency; it did not make sense or reason. We behaved driven by an urgency to return to our native country at any cost or risk. I saw that our actions had contradicted our wisdom; they had obscured our prudence; and they had placed our familiar safety and security in harm's way. We made a decision that changed the direction of my life, and Rangel's life that walks with me now. Thus, we were risking everything not knowing why, in fact, we left. We were moving away from where we had everything to a place where we had to begin from zero again. We were returning to that environment I had left behind for good reasons.

"We got to our native country during in June of 1972; I was hot and rainy period. We arrived and brought with us all of our household belongings. We stayed with my parents' house while a developer built our new house outside the frame of the capital city. I exhausted my daytime running back and forth from my parents' house to the new house, checking the construction progress. We moved right after they delivered the house to us around December 15 of that year."

"You had your house built in fewer than six months; that was fast tracked construction. That construction company must have been in a hurry to finish your house before Christmas."

"Yes, that construction company worked fast; maybe because they build according to pre-designed house models. In fact, they place themselves a goal to finish our house at the beginning of December without us requesting it. I did not know what reasons drove the construction company to fast track the construction of our house. I thought that for some reason things happened, and it was not for me to question their motive; but the construction speed surprised me. I was happy to have our house as soon as possible, and their speed was good for that simple reason. Besides, I was already planning the Christmas Eve dinner at our new house."

"It is a fascinating story; an incredible story. How did you like your new house?"

"The house was fine; we were very happy. We had all the conveniences nearby, excepting, that my parents were distant from our house. I always thought that if anything happened to my parents, it would be difficult for me to get to them in a hurry. It was not possible to have bought a house in their neighborhood; the city was packed and there were no houses or empty lots for sale. I was always thinking of my parents ever since I return; it was as if I had a premonition telling me that I should be attentive to their situation; but I could not distinguish the real reason. It was a strange feeling that could not understand; it did not go away either. It was not homesickness; after all, I have lived in America for several years away from them. Why all of the sudden I felt that way? I did not know.

Chapter 8

My Native Country, a Violent Scenario

1 – The Big Earthquake

"Seven days after we moved in to our new house, a big earthquake destroyed the capital city of that country. The quake damaged our house but it damaged my parents' house even more. The people fled the city and surroundings; they left behind their belongings and their destroyed houses. My parents did not have where to go to take refuge, and we moved them to the new house the morning after that big earthquake. Our native country was in chaos; Rangel took a role in a committee assigned to set up an emergency hospital. That duty kept him occupied almost day and night. I remained alone with time to meditate about the circumstances in the house."

"Your family moved out of your parents' house barely in time. It was a narrow escape, was not it? What did you think about that?"

"Yes it was a close call, but we moved out of my parents' house just in time. My parent's house was inhabitable; it had no roof and the walls were ready to collapse at any moment. My parents spent that night on the street; they had no one else but me to help them. I thought this was the reason we had to leave the United States abruptly. How could I have imagined that my urgency to return to my native country was to be there when my parents needed my help? How could I have thought that the urgency to buy and move to this new house was to provide shelter to my parents after the catastrophe? I found no other reasons than these. I knew then the reason for our crazy return to our country; but I now see that it was not crazy at all. It had a purpose that I could not see at that time. That is how the angels work; they act for a purpose sometimes without warning, but the results come to benefit us. Amid the situation brought about by that earthquake, I thought about our rushed return. I saw my husband and I involved in the decision of returning to our native country. I understood the deep impulses that compelled us to return with no reason despite any cost or risks.

Perhaps, those impulses were the voices of the angels that shouted, 'Return, go back to your country right away.' The reason was to be prepared to support and assist my parents, to care for them after the earthquake, as they took care of me when I lived with them. I saw how the principle of sharing works in life, for the first time. I know that our giving and receiving actions balance at any time. I say that my return to that country was an act of the law of mutual compensation. Life gives to us; life takes from us; if we give love and kindness, we receive love and kindness. It was my time to give assistance and support to my parents. Perhaps, it was my time to credit my account, and Rangel's, who now walks by me, was contributing to that balance. Why Rangel does contribute? He had no obligations. I know that it was my responsibility to help my parents; but for some reason Rangel is with me and his contribution is on his individual account, and that helps me. I could not have done it alone. I know that Rangel is my guardian angel; he stands by me permanently."

"Can you tell us how the angels managed the circumstances to lead you into returning to your native country?"

"I could not say how the angels manipulated the circumstances of our returning to the native land; it was not clear to me. The angels incited our minds and aroused our yearnings; they created nostalgia, caused in us a feeling of urgency, and compelled us to act with no resistance. This time the angels spoke into my thoughts and my husband's. Why was Rangel involved? Could it be that he is my guardian angel, indeed, who always walks with me? That is too much to ask, is it not? We tied our lives, and his decisions and mine are mutual. In similar manner, the things that concern me also concern him; in particular, we include the cost and benefits of our acts. I saw an important fact coming out of our return to native country. That is, my parents and my relatives got all the benefits from it whereas; Rangel or his relatives did not get any. I studied the sequence of events in this episode and concluded that we had returned to that country for one purpose; that is, helping my parents.

After the quake, we lived through the shortages of those days until the situation normalized a day at a time. We chose to adjust to the situation as fast as we could; we thought there was nothing we could have done to prevent that natural catastrophe.

2 – A New Friend Appeared, Aida

"Misti, you have said that you believe that something happens for a purpose; you said that something that had happened most of the time was something good in your favor. What can you say about this big event?"

"In general, Miguel, one thinks and says about these catastrophes that it is the Divine will of God, and we can do nothing. On the morning following that horrific tragedy, the tremors were still coming in sequence; we all had awful feelings that an even bigger quake would strike. The people fled from the city and from our urban development to places far from the area of destruction. At early hours of the morning of that earthquake day, we realized that we were alone. The people fled from our vicinity, excepting a young woman, Aida, and her four years old child in a house across the street from mine; Carlos, a boy left by himself guarding a hardware store business about half a block away. We found no markets or stores around; we had no water, electric power, or telephones. We had nothing besides solitude, fear, ashes floating in the air and a smell of smoke from fires. We smelled a whiff of dead bodies from within the city core, which along with a fear of another bigger earthquake, filled us with fears. We had two propane gas tanks for cooking, but we did not have enough food to last three days. That boy, Carlos, had a freezer with meat and chicken. I cooked for us remaining in our neighborhood block. In that situation, I met that young woman, Aida. We stayed there with my parents and my grandmother; we support each other, caring for the children, and sleeping on makeshift beds on the sidewalks some distance away from the houses. We were afraid of the aftershock tremors that kept coming. Aida and I started a sincere friendship with solidarity; we shared and gave mutual support while we lived in that neighborhood. She facilitated her husband's property about twelve miles outside the city. We bathed there, and we brought water back to the house. We gave her shelter and food we all prepared in my kitchen. We, Aida and I, began our friendship in that neighborhood; we had a condition full of uncertainties, hardships, and need. Rangel and I had moved my parents to my house before the masses began looting the city and neighborhoods.

"The city had reached to a new normality, day by day, several months later. I say new normality because it was not possible to bring back that city that was before the earthquake in a short time.

"The government fenced off the entire city placing it of limits; they took possession of the properties within those limits a few weeks later. My parents lost their house to the confiscation process ordered. I had a better understanding of the actions of the angels after all those events. I have no doubts the angels exist and work with defined purposes; they work with subtle and delicate manners most of the time and in other occasions in a drastic way. I live observing when the angels send their signs or messages, speaking to us in their silent language. The question, 'which event will be next following that massive cataclysm' kept coming back to my mind. I wanted to know beforehand; I wanted to be in control of the steps in my life. I wanted no other hands weaving the embroidering of my life. I wanted the freedom to choose threads, drawings, lines, and colors that knitted the picture of my life in that embroidering. I wanted to make my decisions, select the threads, and make the knots and moorings of my embroidering. I wanted to be the one that assigns the hands that reach out awaiting another hand, making up a future connection. What had happened in my country was horrific; it was scary. I did not expect that earthquake, and did not imagine the magnitude of its consequences. There were over ten thousand dead and three quarter of a million persons fled the city. Yes, I understood the clear urgency of going back to the native country. The angels gave us enough time to buy a lot, build, and move to our house before that earthquake destroyed my parent's house. The urgency of going back to our country was obvious then; I thank the Lord for the realization of that return to my native land in time."

"How or why do events happen?"

"Events happen on their own; although, we may influence the circumstances that make an event, to certain limited extent. Nobody gives enough time to think about the reasons behind an event. I am sure that if we look up the causes and effects of any event we may find its true purpose. There are random and driven events. Random events have no specific purpose for us; at least we see them that way. These events come out of the mix of circumstances, following no pattern or plan. Driven events have their set purpose; and they come about because of managed circumstances. A random or a driven event may yield its own derivative events, called accidental events; these are no part of a plan but rather arise by chance as side effects of those events.

"Almost a year after that earthquake my parents bought a new house around the perimeter of the core of the destroyed city. Our insurance paid for the repairs of our house by that time, and we, my family, continued living in it. During that time, the friendship with Aida and her children grew stronger."

3 – The Abduction of My Husband

"Was the environment in your native country safe?"

"I felt a growing tension in the country and I did not know what was. It asked, 'what holds the future for us?' The economy of that country had not recovered after three years from the day of that earthquake. I felt that the conditions were brewing a new change that I could not understand. The corruption in the government went out of control. The number of new businesses, owned and ran by public officials, grew larger and larger in those three years. Fair competition in the market became rare; the public officials did not abide by that. The public sector was taking down the private sector. My husband thought of that situation as a paralyzing stage. Although I did not understand what he meant; but I noticed that domestic supplies were scarce in the market, including medicines. The country became hostile; and a feeling of civil displeasure grew all around. People talked about a revolution; they said that an armed movement had started up in the mountains. A few months later, on father's day, I woke up with a rare feeling. My husband and boys were getting ready to go to the nearby business center to get certain things we needed. They went so well dressed that I said, 'Careful, they may snatch you guys.' They went in the car and after about thirty or forty minutes my children returned by themselves on foot. 'Where is your father?' I asked them. They said, 'mammy, they kidnapped him. 'For a moment, I thought it was Rangel's joke; however, I began to worry accepting that it was true when I saw my children's seriousness, did not see the car on the street and I did not see Rangel. I asked, 'where is the car?' My boys said they had taken the car with them. Until that moment, my boys began crying. I went with my brother and children to the place where they abducted my husband to verify that action. A young man was there who knew Rangel, and had taken the license plate number of the kidnapper's car. A man witnessed what happened and said that the kidnapers got out the car with machine guns and by force, pushing and shoving, took my husband with them. This event was an abrupt change for us. I felt that something of harmful was happening. My whole family, in first place my brother, involved themselves in what was happening with no doubts. We told the news media what was happening. I knew that Rangel had joined several professional organizations; we asked these for their support at the same time. Rangel's brothers and sisters, nephews and nieces and the rest of his relatives at once got involved in locating him. At noon of that day, the news reported that the authorities did apprehend my husband; the reporter did not say where they had him. Those who knew my husband came to express their support. Many of them said that we should act fast because the authorities could declare him missing without a trace. Hours of anguish, uncertainty, and fear, reigned in the house. That same morning, we began looking for a lawyer. Some said to have no time; others said that their experience was not in political cases. Some others said they could not take my husband case because they had tendencies against the government. In fact, an armed revolution against the government had started in the mountains and in the cities. Rangel's case was as a ping-pong ball bouncing from lawyer to lawyer until we found one willing to take Rangel's case. This lawyer had a long background and an ample experience in cases of this type.

"Every day we made new efforts to find him, and each night we had new anguishes and sleeplessness. Fears of not seeing him anymore assaulted me. At last, they allowed Rangel a personal public appearance. They accused him of conspiring against the government of that country at the beginning of the case. An accusation such as this was a common method during those days and thus, it was not a surprise that they found Rangel guilty. We appealed the case the same day, and the court found Rangel innocent and exonerated him of all charges two weeks later. Nevertheless, some people said that my husband's life was in danger. It was no longer safe for Rangel to remain in that country."

"Why do you say it was not safe anymore? Is not that a free country?"

"No, it was not safe and it was not a free country. The lawyers advised us that Rangel should leave the country right after his was set free. They said that Rangel faced the chance of an accidental elimination if he stayed in the city. Thus, he came out free, unharmed and in good health during the early evening. Rangel left the country well protected in the early hours of the following day. My children and I stayed at my parent's new house, but by now had planned to meet my husband a few days later.

"What a case, Misti, what violence."

"I could not understand many things of this story. I thought about the terms, conditions and adjustments to leave my house in safe hands; but after that, I meditated on the reasons of my relocation. I felt as if this scenario wanted to expel us from its domain, 'but why?' What happened to Rangel puzzled me. I was aware of no reason, but that was its purpose. For some odd reason, I have to think that we had to abandon the country, and the one thing that came to my mind was that the tasks in my native country had concluded. We had to go to a new position from where we would fulfill the following node of the embroidering of my life. I cannot stop thinking that all those circumstances and event were acts of the angels. They managed the conditions that expelled my family out of that country. Without a doubt, it would be a conceit or arrogance of mine to think that everything had happened for me at that time. No, that could not be, and I think that those conditions applied to me, to my family and the general population. Other individuals were involved in this case that receive their own reward. The reality was that everyone affected by the result of that event underwent a change of the course of his or her life at the same time. I saw that the angels executed this event with violence; was it required? The angels had to set all parts for this change away from the brink of doubts. I thought that the method employed and what happened had to obliterate all feelings or desires in us to stay in that country. Again, I thought, it this is the work of the angels, I am nobody to challenge their reasoning. I had to concede that they know what they are doing since they knew the road and ending of my journey."

Chapter 9

Living in a Neighboring Country

1 – Why We Move to the Neighboring Country.

"Where did your husband go?"

"Rangel had to get out of my native country immediately after his release; and the best solution was for him to go a neighboring country and wait there for me and the children. Rangel got a job in that neighboring country the night before to his departure. One of his brothers gave Rangel a job at his brother's company branch in that neighboring country. Rangel was to manage the company brach in that country; he was not moving to that neighboring country empty handed."

"Do you think the angels hurt you to accomplish their purpose if necessary?"

"I did not think that their means justify their purpose. Nevertheless, from the results I saw, that the angels did not intend to hurt us; they may have caused us anguishes and sufferings, but at the same time, they provided us with means that mitigated our pain and suffering. I asked could it be that their strategy is to play with my situation. Would they play with the circumstances surrounding me? It was difficult for me to understand the purpose of those events. I knew that they had changed the course of my life abruptly, changing the drawing and colors of the embroidering of my life at the same time. After all, what could I do on my own, with my own choices, to change the circumstances that structured that event? It seems that the angels excluded me from their decision making process; they lead me on a way that took me through an exit-gate within the circumstances at hand and the time available. Few days after Rangel had left, we gathered all the things we could and traveled to join him in that neighboring country.

"Those harrowing days had gone by; and after we had accommodated to that new environment, I reviewed the events that pushed us out our native land. I recognized the conditions and the angels in this story, as I had done before. In this case, an entire scenario turned against us. It seemed to me that he angels wanted to seal off that scenario; perhaps they wanted to leave just one exit for Rangel to abandon the country. My brother, Marcus, told me to call the news media and denounce the abduction of my husband on that morning. He asked me if Rangel was a member of any professional association; and I said yes. He then told me to call them right away to inform them of what happened to my husband. The associations did not waste any time; they issued their own statements demanding the authorities to let the public see my husband state of being. The news reported during those days the abduction of my husband by armed men working for the government. It was a spontaneous act making a demand in a single voice. The angels guided us to a lawyer to handled Rangel's case while we searched for a suitable lawyer for the case, surprising me with the way they did it. This lawyer was about to go out of that country. Once we found this lawyer, we knew that we could not have found him had we had taken a longer search; he took our case. I did let him know that my family included American citizens and USA residents. I thought that this fact was important for Rangel's defense. Rangel's brother offered him a job in that neighboring country of his own free will. This job stabilized the situation for Rangel in that new country.

"As a final point, I say that the angels acted through several persons that came into support the actions of that event. Amongst them, I saw the man who waited for us at the kidnapping place with valuable information for us. This case was one major event that changed the course of my life. I saw that several forces and influences conspired indeed to kick us out that country. I saw that those associations played an important role in this case. I understood the purpose of their action. They came out in support of Rangel at the right time. They were threads weaved and left waiting to connect, and they moored in the embroidering by making that declaration. Those were the circumstances of a general plan to relocate us from that country to a neighboring one. That native country was a hostile scenario and it did not have a place for us in it. All threads and strings that pictured that episode of my life were weaved into the embroidering of my life. I mentioned of my life because, for me, my husband was and still is the guardian angel who accompanies me. Besides the above, I saw that the angels knew that my parents would need my help after that earthquake; the purpose of my returning to my native country was helping my parents when they needed my support. Of course, I had to follow my way with Rangel and my family, wherever that way might take my family and me in life. I did not see it, but I am sure that I would see it with time."

2 – My life in that neighboring country

"How was the environment of that other country? Did you ever settle?"

"Our life was a normal life in that neighboring country; however, something was missing. In fact, it was an isolated life for us although my husband had close relatives in that country. The roots of Rangel showed that he was an international person. We rented a house in a top, middle class, development, but for me, it was a confinement; it filled my life with solitude. I lived alone with my children there most of the time; Rangel had to travel to his work in remote places where communication facilities were still unavailable for weeks at a time. The days were passing by, the months, and, after almost three years, I had not adjusted to that scenario. It was a strange contradictory situation because the country was a nice place with a high cultural, social level and political stability. Why I did not adapt to this environment I ignored. Many anguishing thoughts came to my mind that made me restless and unsettled. I began to yearn for living in a secure and stable place; I wished to return to America. We had been traveling to the United States every year, but it was insufficient to go there for a short time. I needed security and peace, freedom of choice and social relations at a work place. I thought that a job would be a therapy for me after living alone isolated in that house. I thought about how important it would be for me to interact with other people. I felt that a job was necessary for my mental health. A job would allow me to engage in other activities such as dialogues other than I have with my family nature.

"The economy of that country was bleak; it had entered a downward spiral. I could not think of looking for a job there. Rangel's job was coming to end in sixty days and he did not have new projects. When I meditated about that situation, impartially, I analyzed it, at least I tried; but I felt as if my head was being packed swelling with ideas against staying in that country.

"I found something I did not like about our stay in that country every day. We could no longer live in that situation, and we planned to sell our household goods and return to America. I think that the economic situation in this country did force out our decision to leave that country; however, the angels stuffed my head with ideas, ideas that had a major influence in that decision. For me, this episode was another manifestation, a clear and loud message of the angels in my way; they advised me to get out of that neighboring country as soon as possible. Those voices said almost shouting that neighboring country was no place for my family and me. We did not have to be there, and the evidences were clear. I did not see any other choice than the one to return to America."

"Misti, your situation was difficult. What did you do?"

"We rushed to advertise our household goods for sale on a local newspaper. We scheduled the sale to start at six in the morning of a Saturday of that winter of 1980. I was surprised to see people coming in the early evening hours of the day before to pick, choose, and buy what they could. The people lined up on the sidewalk the following morning to enter my house. We sold everything, expensive things, fine things, simple things; they even picked up and bought my husband's work muddy boots. We sold the bar supply, scotch whiskeys, liquor bottle lots, imported and national rum bottles, and wines. We sold the dining room, cookware, bedroom sets, even my children's toys, excepting some toys Keith did not want to sell. We sold everything in a blinking of an eye. It happened that way and it was real; by the mid-morning of that Saturday, we had sold everything already. By the afternoon of that day, the house was empty. 'It is something crazy, unbelievable.' I said in the deafening echo of that empty house. I screamed with joy and awe, 'Could you believe that this country entered an economic recession? Can they buy as this in a recession?' One can say that this was another stroke of luck, but I do not agree with that. I saw a sequence of activities in the event that was precise, in action and timing, to reach its purpose. That purpose set the basis for our return to America. I say that the angels managed the circumstances to set up that basis. The angels could not endure no failure or obstacles 'why was it anyway as that?"

"Indeed this story is remarkable. I could not believe that you sold an entire household belonging in fewer than six hours. I trust you and I know it was true because you experienced it. I agree with you that it is incomprehensible how the people could spend in a recession that fast."

Chapter 10

Final Return to America

1 – How that Return Was Possible

"My husband maintained contact with friends in the United States, and traveled alone to a state in the southern part of America; he had a job possibility there. Meanwhile, I needed to resolve certain things before we travel to join him. We could not travel with him at the same time. Perhaps, the master plan included my staying behind so I could travel first to my parents' country. My parents' economic situation was forcing them to sell their house and did not have any place to go. I had to end my house rental agreement, in order that my parents could move into my house. I did not have any problem; the tenant accepted to terminate the rental agreement asking for some time to find another place. The tenant found a place in two weeks and moved out right away. I took care of that, and my parents moved themselves to my house in that country. I had no problem ending the rental agreement; and I asked myself, 'why the solutions of my hardships are simple, fast, and easy, why?' Perhaps as always, one could say that it was another stroke of luck; however, I say, no it is not. I thought the angels in my way managed things to protect me. It seemed they did not have time to waste in their timetable.

"The chapter of my life in those countries took eight years to open and close, but those years were a negligible time in the infinite existence. With that, I confirmed once more, that actions and results leading to complete a mission assigned to me is what counts. I went on thinking for many weeks about the conditions that forced my family to get out of that country. I felt as if my history were repeating itself with all its episodes and chapters. It was the second scenario that expelled us, as that of my parents' country. That scenario pushed us out so we could go back to America for some reasons. I could not say that this happened because I had wished it. I would say that the economic situation of that country was out of my control. I thought that the angels had planned this event for us to go back to America. I knew that the reason for this event would come in the future. The circumstances conspired to take us back to America; did it have to be America? This was the angels' real intentions. One could say that we came during the down cycle of that country. The economy of poor countries oscillates from good to bad times faster than rich countries. I thought that was not the case; I think that there is always a purpose in each change of the course in my life. We must be careful in studying the purpose; it shows up at the conclusion of an event. I always think about the trend of a purpose to anticipate what may come next; that is, a coming event that will link with it. I reviewed those circumstances, and I identified the angels that came to help me in this case. There is no question in my mind that the angels had their paws in the result of that event; I was sure that would understand as time goes on."

2 – Aida, My Unexpected Angel

"What can you tell us about your return to America? Did somebody wait for you there? Did you have second thoughts?"

"No, nobody waited for us there. We had no second thoughts about our decision of going back to America. The situation in that neighboring country turned hostile for us to stay there. Let me tell you, I had identified the circumstances and the angels in this episode of my journey. First, I noted that the economy of that country played the main role in the story of our returning to the United States. I did not matter if my husband had continued working there. For me, Aida was the lead character in this story; she had moved with her children to the United States in 1980. In this occasion, she extended her hands to give us the support we needed. I ignored that Aida had left with his children to America. I found out of her move when I went back to my native country after my husband had left; later, when I spoke with Rangel I told him that Aida was in a western state of the United States. Rangel got a negative result from that work promise he had in that southern state. This circumstance forced him to go to that western state from which we had left when we return to my native country in 1972. Later, but in fewer than thirty days after my husband had left, I traveled to join him in that western state of America. I left my children with Mariel and Eddy, their aunt and uncle, in that neighboring country so we may have time to settle in USA. Rangel got in touch with Aida, and she offered her help, lodging us in her house while we re-establish a stable situation. Aida was a key thread in the weave of the embroidering of my life. If we had gone to any other state, we did not know what circumstances would have been. For me, Aida was an angel that moved to America as a piece in a chess game, and waited available to help us with our return. I know there is a mutual compensation, as I have explained before. We had helped Aida during the earthquake in my native country. Now Aida tends her hand to us. I think Aida was the instrument the angel used to facilitate this new change in my life, now, with my children and Rangel. I also saw the strategy of the action plan that guided my return and the causes that create it. The degrading economy, Rangel's job that was ending soon, and the lack of public projects in that country were parts of their plan. Third, the fast sale of the household belongings, and forth, the unfilled work prospect. Fifth, the fast dissolution of the rental agreement of my house, and sixth, my parent's relocation to my house in that country came just in time. I was amazed to see that the coincidences of those circumstances favored my wishes; and, I could think of nothing other than the defined purpose I followed guided by my angels."

"When did you bring your children?"

"My children came a few days later, and at last, we were together again. I was happy."

"Now that you were back in USA, did you maintain your desire to work?"

3 – How I got My Final Employment

"Yes, of course. I felt a great desire to work so I could create my own financial resource. I did not clearly know why I wanted to create such resource. A few days after our return, Aida's husband offered me his help with getting a job in the insurance company where he worked. He made an interview for me with Mister Chuck, the district office manager. I went to that interview and Mister Chuck gave me the job after a short conversation. This event was surreal; I went, we met and got the job. It was that fast and easy; it was unbelievable. It seemed to me as if they had agreed beforehand about giving me that job and were just waiting for my arrival. It was that simple. I started my work that next Monday following my interview. I could not believe that I got a job roughly one week after I had returned to America. Perhaps it was another stroke of luck, one may say, and it may be, but the process was similar to the process of those events that I have told up to now. There is still more; Aida offered me her car, so I could go to my work daily. She said that her husband would take her to her work place every day while I used her car. Aida and her husband were both generous and altruistic in their own ways. I admire, respect, and thank both of them for their sincere gesture of friendship that forever placed me in a debt with her. I have to repay this debt in the future, even though I did not know when. The story related to my work had many facets. For example, looking for work is hard, but angels appeared in my way and worked hard to manage the circumstances so I could find a job. I have learned that not all is roses and candies. That job required me to drive a long distance on those high-speed highways to and from work, and the complicated work tasks were so stressing that I wanted to resign in the first days. It was so bad indeed that I cried every day; I often told my husband that I could not cope with that work. Perhaps, if I have had my freedom of choice I had left that work at that time.

"However, my husband, Aida's husband, Mister Chuck, and the circumstances, they gave me their reasons to keep the job. I felt as if they would not let me resign, and in a certain way, they were compelling me to stay. The office district manager offered me time for learning those procedures; thus, I remain in the job he gave me.

4 – An Angel, My Friend Doris Came.

"The job was so demanding that my body trembled with fear in route to my work every day. One day, I was going in to work committed to resigning, when a new office manager, Doris, appeared in the office. Even before we introduced that morning, she tapped my shoulder calling me to a private room; she said, 'I will teach you the business procedures and handling of office work.' I saw how this episode developed; and that excited and relieved me. I have no doubts that the angels had managed the minds of the manager and office manager to make my situation; they made my work easier. My nerves improved somehow; however, I still had to deal with my fears of driving back and forth to work daily. I wanted to quit the work for that driving, but nobody would support me with that decision. One day I talked to Doris about my fears, and she encouraged me again distracting me with her advices and stories. Doris was endearing to me, and I like her trusting attitude towards me; days later, she trusted me that her older daughter had died a few weeks before, and

I reminded her of her daughter. Thus, a new friendship was starting for me, a connection, a new mooring in the embroidering of my life.

"All these circumstances resolving my situation were, indeed, they were the work of my angels. Did they handle my work situation to keep me in my job? Did the angels handle the circumstances that way, did them not? I placed the highlights of this story on the precision of the timing of each action. I saw how the events followed one another to shape the result, my new job. These events could not have happened by an act of chance. The events I have narrated in my stories have happened for a definite purpose. However, I saw the purpose until the next event happened; until then I saw the connection between events. I have seen that the pattern of purposes of those events showed a tendency; they showed a direction or destiny. That tendency marked my path to the end of my journey and painted the picture of my mission in the embroidering of my life. I admit that it frightened me to have seen the exact timing and ease with which the evens have happened. I had to think that somebody planned and directed the actions and events; and I say that because they happened when and where I need a definite result. I think that everybody have had similar events including the author of this book; although nobody may have noticed the influence or have observed them as I have done. I ask, 'can these events be strokes of luck? How can that be?' They could be strokes of luck; however, when the events follow a consistent sequence with a clear purpose revealed in days ahead; when those threads, those hands, prepared in anticipation to tie ahead, and their results confirmed that purpose, it is easy to conclude that it is not luck. This is how I interpret my experiences. The sequence of events that have experienced showed that the sequence had an intention. This sequence had an objective. The objective in this story was to keep me in that job even though I did not know their reason yet. By that time, I did not worried about; I knew that I would know why ahead in time.

5 – How We Bought the First Car

"One Saturday morning, Rangel brought from the store a newspaper; it was unusual because he did not buy newspapers. We read that an agency advertised used cars for sale with no down payment and no credit required. We went and picked a Chevrolet car, a model Montecarlo. The agent processed the paperwork, and we drove that car home the same afternoon. It was a neat car, eight cylinders, two doors, pale green, white leather seats, etcetera. Thankfully, we told Aida we were not going to need her car anymore because Rangel had bought one. We resolved our transportation problem; now Aida's husband no longer had to take her to her work every day. I asked, 'was this another stroke of luck, could it be?' Everything had gone so smoothly that it surprised me. Perhaps I did not have to be surprised; after all, I have had many cases like this happening in previous stories. I thought about what had incited my husband to buy the newspaper; I wondered about what guided us to see that car dealer's advertising that morning. We were not looking for a car, but the advertising compelled us to inquire. The agency processed our application and approved our loan in less than two hours; the entire process was as easy as saying hello. 'It was not a standard procedure,' I thought. It was so easy that I could say it was a deliberate move to sell us that car no matter what. They could have not possibly verified our employment one a Saturday to say the least. Looking back to how this event happened, I had to think that my angels managed the purchase of our car; and we solved our transportation problem."

"It was simple indeed, can you tell us more?"

"My stories are not finished yet. Let me say that behind a surprise, another one appeared. My big surprise was the frequency with which the events happened in my life; and this story was not different. We did not wait long before we both were working again in America. Rangel got a job with a company to do plant engineering. He started to work about a month after I had started at my job. Our income topped our expenditures at the time we spent the balance of the funds we had brought with us; and as usual, the circumstances and events engaged exactly in time to protect us.

6 – How We Rented the Apartment

"For me, each episode of the journey of my life seemed difficult at its beginning; it was because, as ignorant mortal of what was coming, I was frightened by the uncertainties of the moment. Somehow, the situations spun to give me what I needed. We looked for a place to move to as soon as our financial situation normalized. We found an unfurnished, two bedrooms apartment that we could afford, about two months later. I recalled that the agreement to rent the apartment had restrictions we did not meet. They allowed one master bedroom for a couple, one bedroom for two boys or one girl. We did not meet the requirements because we had two boys and one girl; nevertheless. The apartment manager waved the requirements, and she wrote two children in the rental agreement; but she let us bring my girl and two boys. It was an unfurnished apartment, and we needed to get all basic items for it on an urgent basis. We bought items of immediate need such as beds and bedding; but we delayed other items such as kitchenware and furniture for later. I understood that we have desires and needs that are beyond reach, if we do not have the resources to get them. In my experiences, resources have not been obstacles, and I emphasized that point in my stories. I have had experiences that scared me, because I did not understand why they happened. I did not know their origin, as I describe in the following stories. I learned something valuable in my life; when I yearned for something with humility accepting that it might not appear it appears. Things may take a long time to come by because certain conditions must converge for them to appear. I knew that we needed resources besides our own to meet the conditions of that event; but I understood that resources are not enough to get the result. I have seen that specific circumstances merged to yield an event; this was true in particular when that event had a short time frame. That was our case when we were re-settling in America back then. As I said before, we took an unfurnished apartment and we needed to furnish it as soon as possible. I thought that preserving foods for the family was more important than getting a car. I thought that it was urgent for us to get a refrigerator. I mentioned that Aida lend me her car to go to work while her husband took her to work. I had been aware that the order in which we yearn for things perhaps is not the order in which they may come. The appearance of things conforms to the circumstances that must take place for things to appear. We do not control the circumstances; I believe the angels manipulate them in the easiest way possible to make the things to appear. I yearned for having comfort in the house and a car for transport. I sighed with resignation and watched my humble yearnings grow; I had no arrogance or desperation. I will explain in my next stories, what I am referring to at this time.

7 – How I Received a Refrigerator

"About three weeks after we had moved to the apartment, I arrived at work as always, quiet, and calm. Indeed, I am shy by nature; I do not disclose my private and personal things. That morning,

I was in the office's lunchroom, getting a cup of coffee, when Doris arrived. After she greeted me, and without roundups, she asked me, 'Misti, does your apartment come with gas kitchen range?' 'Yes, Doris, I answered her'; in fact, it comes with kitchen range but with no refrigerator. 'Good', she said with excitement, I have one brand new refrigerator that I have not been able to make it work. It must have some control to start it up, who knows where. She said, 'I do not want it because I bought another one. Do you need a refrigerator?' She asked. 'Yes, I need one,' I answered. 'Do you want it?' She asked. 'Sure, I want it' I said with pleasant surprise. 'Come to see it at my house,' she said. I said, 'OK, I will come this Saturday.' I poured my cup of coffee and returned to my desk. I thought about how things happened, coincidence or not; the thing I needed appeared, without me asking or looking for it and at the precise moment. What could I say? It came by itself through Doris; nevertheless, she did not know that I needed a kitchen or a refrigerator when she asked, and she had one of each. In fact, I needed a refrigerator; she had an extra one to give, and, without my asking for it, Doris offered it to me one. I could not believe this happening; was it an act of fate? I did not think so; there were too many precise coincidences to be luck. I believe that my angels managed the situation to produce a solution that helped me. This event was too precise in time to be a coincidence in those circumstances. It happened that way; and Rangel and I went to Doris's house the Saturday of that week. I said, 'what a surprise, it is yellow like the color of my kitchen's accessories.' Indeed, the refrigerator was new, as Doris had said, without sign of any use; it still had the plastics wrappings and packing they bring from the factory. 'We will take it,' I said, 'how much do you want for it?' I asked Doris. 'Nothing', she said, 'it is my gift to you for your apartment,' she answered. We stayed with Doris for a couple of hours before we drove back to the apartment with the refrigerator with us. On the way back, we talked about how an item that we needed the most came so easily.

"Strange things happen in life, a refrigerator that came out of the air without anticipation; was it the answer to my yearning? I thought that it was that, because that is how the angels handled circumstances making up an event. For me, Doris was an angel delivering on time the item I most needed. I must say my husband repaired the control switch that did not let it start; however, I had a brand new refrigerator working. This story made me think about the causalities of my life; that is a subtle form whereupon the angels seem to help me on my way. Doris did not know I needed a refrigerator, but her action had the same content I had in my yearning. This is the pivotal point of my story. I thought the angels guided Doris into offering me a kitchen range or a refrigerator; indeed, she did not know I needed one of these. Nevertheless, I thanked God and my angels for what had happened.

8 – How we bought my Furniture

"Two days after we got the refrigerator, Rangel returned home after work, and he said 'I have a surprise, do you want to know?' When I heard what my husband said my head spun thinking about how could that be? I could not believe what Rangel told me. He said that a fellow engineer, Manuel, met him in their workplace vault room asked him if he needed a dining room, and a living room set, as soon as he entered the room. Rangel asked him about the condition of that furniture, and Manuel said that they were new, wood, and metal. Manuel had to get rid of those items to make room in his apartment because his father was coming to live with him. I asked Rangel, 'what, a dining room and living room furniture set?' 'Yes', Rangel answered. I could not believe it; we needed those items to complete furnishing our apartment. It was another surprise of my angels' play; we had gone through the emotions of acquiring a car and receiving a refrigerator and we received one more. When I got out of this new surprise, I asked Rangel, 'how much does he wants for his furniture?' He responded, 'Manuel said to pay him what I believe is reasonable; he must sale that furniture quickly or he will donate it to the Good Will. We must decide by tomorrow, because his father comes next Monday'. My fear grew more because, under pressure, we had no time to think about this investment. The days went by, and Saturday arrived faster than usual or, so it seemed. These furniture circumstances kept me astonished up to that day. We, my husband the children and I, went to see those items. I did not want to illusion myself too much because illusions are only that. Surprisingly, everything was so timely that it did not seem real; it was beyond the realm of coincidences. As one may say, it was too good to be true. We needed three items, a car, a refrigerator, and furniture, and they all appeared on their own. It is true I yearned for that furniture, but I neither looked for them nor told anyone we needed them. I do not want to say that we should not do anything on our own; but we should rest assure that if we humbly yearn for something that something will show up. We arrived at Manuel's place, and I met him.

He was a young man, humorous, active, and his wife centered and happy. They both invited us to have lunch with them. Manuel acted as if he knew us for years, friendly and open. My husband and Manuel arranged the sales as they did. We loaded the furniture on a trailer we rented, said bye and returned home. The dining set was a chromed metal and glass table with six chairs. The sofa was eight feet, brown, velvet like material. An armchair and a center table with two lamp tables completed the set.

"Seating on the new sofa in the apartment, we went over the last events of that afternoon. My husband said to me that Manuel would take whatever we could pay him because he had to get rid of that furniture any way. My husband paid him a fair amount. We remained with those thoughts amazed; we had gotten an almost new, excellent quality, furniture set, and a new friendship. I thought about the purpose and way that Manuel came on to offer us the furniture, but it did not make sense; this furniture event happened fast and without precedents. My husband said to me two months later that Manuel had left his work. He had no opportunity to wishing him well. New thoughts of possible chances and purposes came to my mind again; thus, I began to analyze that phenomenon. Let me see, Manuel met my husband that morning and offered Rangel the furniture; we saw it and bought it, and Manuel disappeared afterward forever. This sequence is too straightforward to result from an act of fate, luck, or coincidence; we had an eminent need of those items to be satisfied within a definite time. I thought that Manuel's function were within the angels' work. We looked for Manuel in the place where he lived, but he no longer lived there, and he had left without leaving a forwarding address. This story increased my experiences; now I think that Manuel appeared in life bringing help to us when we needed, and after rendering his help, he continued on his way. The angels work in that way; they come, they help, they leave expecting no rewards or praises. If you think about, you may say that the angels work is indifferent to human feelings; and I say 'no,' on the contrary, the angels show kindness and love for us. Assume that a stranger extends a helping hand to you when you needed help, and then the stranger continues on his or her way. Would not you think the stranger acted of pure love and kindness for a fellow human? This is the role of a true guardian angel. The stranger does not know you and does not get any benefit from helping you. For me, the angels assigned Manuel to find us, help us, provide the things we needed and disappear afterwards. This is incredible, but it is true; what remained behind in our memories was a name, Manuel, and a furniture set in the apartment. The memories and the furnishing were evidences and proof that the angels in my way lived in my story. In this story of the furniture, Manuel was the means to achieve the angels' work. The results of this event were reasonable and real. I found no pieces out of place in the chain of occurrences. Thus, I concluded that it was an act of the angels in my way. The act of that dog preventing my step to death, and the appearance of the household items were similar, and that frighten me. These events seemed to occur just for my benefit, and they frightened me, because, I thought, they could come against me someday. We had all we need now to go on our way, self-supported with jobs, housing, and the rest.

"I think that I must be kind and perform righteous deeds to compensate and to earn the love and kindness of God and the angels in my way. I have mentioned that there is a principle of mutual compensation in life. This principle is an account of personal deeds good and bad that remains in balance. When something bad happened to you, something good happens to you later; that is the balance. If you insult your fellows, they will insult you; if you hate them, they will hate you; but if you love them, they will love you back. This is the base of peaceful coexistence. I think that if I do only good deeds my life will settle in an everlasting happiness. I think that this attitude is the key that opens the door of our soul to our angels; and we will reduce or eliminate our negative elements such as egotism and greed.

"One more chapter of my life closed; but in reviewing those events, I saw the threads, drawings, lines, and colors weaving the embroidering in my life. The event in this story merged so I could finish another part of the picture on the embroidering of my life. It is the basis of my settling from which I remain ready to perform the next phase of the journey in the mission of my life. The threads weaving the embroidering did not show the entire picture yet. My embroidering still had loose yarns waiting for other yarns that will add other moorings and ties ahead in time. For instance, we had no chance to return Manuel's obvious generosity; he is no longer around and we do not know his whereabouts. Nevertheless, he opened a debit account for us with the rest of the world that we must credit as required along the path of our lives. 'Can you understand, Miguel, why I say that?' I know you do, nevertheless let me say that I believe there is a mutual compensation process in life. This process controls the accounting of our giving and taking in our lives. I believe in this mutual compensation, and I am sure that by giving more, I receive more attention and help from angels in my way. I must deposit in my account a value equal to the value of Manuel's deed to balance it. My theory is that the angels provide us with means, methods, and resources to fulfill our mission whatever this may be. My angels gave me those conveniences, and in turn, I remained able and willing to fulfill my mission. The angels managed the circumstances to get the results that met the purposes of my mission; they excluded casual results that hindered or delayed that goal. In my stories, I have emphasized that right after an event closed; another one began without my asking for it. This is so, because there must not be gaps in history. I see that my life has followed a path with no time to spare, and each activity has had the exact time to develop and produce a result. In other words, our lives must go on with no delays regardless of the circumstances or conditions of the event that just ended. I always thought about the next event, what could it be? Overcoming the fears that these experiences caused in me, I let the angels lead my path. I know that I had to participate in the management of my life; and I have contributed in the making of the events that write up its story. I have worked in the weaving of the picture on the embroidering of my mission; because weaving the picture of the mission of my life on the embroidering, I included moorings and ties that advanced it to its end."

"It seemed that your life was exciting and dynamic. Did you adapt to your work."

9 – *Strange Relocation of My Company*

"Driving on that, heavy traffic, and high-speed freeway stressed me; do you remember I mentioned that? Well, without my knowing how or why, the district office where I worked relocated to a building across the street from where we lived. How could I have believed that such relocation happened to help me? In fact, that move eliminated my need to drive to and from work daily. I could not stop thinking about the reasons that made that company move their offices. I thought that it was not because of my nerves, because I had conquered and controlled my fears for a certain time already. For me, it was a blessing and a relief of my fearful situation, because, I no longer had to drive that distance. Besides, having my work across the street from my apartment was a strange advantage for me; I was able to pick up my children at school, bring them home, and stayed with them for a while during my break hour. Nobody else at work gained that much convenience. I mentioned that, in this life, we give up something and take something in exchange. In this story, a sad part was that Doris was no longer with the company. She had retired before the office relocated to its new place across the street from my apartment. My time at work with Doris was short, but my friendship with Doris grew more after her retirement. She was much older than I was, and in some occasions, I looked as her adopted daughter, as she used to call me. I felt a deep gratitude for her, and I visited Doris to see her and share with her part of my time, whenever I could. I thought that any attention I could give her was little to repay her for what she did for me."

"Misti, where do you place Doris in your story?

"Doris was a key person in this story. I think that if she had not arrived I would have resigned that work, for sure. In truth, I owe Doris my job. It seems that Doris came to teach me and stayed sufficient time for my complete learning before she retired. Is it not amazing? She was in retirement and she came back as trainer. She taught me well; I learned from her the best office management methods, and procedures for that insurance office chain. I learned the principles and ethics required to become one of the best employees at that work. Thanks to her training and advices, I became a capable employee in my work. Mister Chuck recognized my capacity to learn, and he was pleased with my work performance. I learn from him the strict agent's procedures and ethics for a district office of that company. The role Doris played in this story was similar to the role Manuel played in that furniture story. The difference between these two cases is that Doris did not disappear the way Manuel did. Doris, as Manuel, was an angel in my way that showed up to help me and then she stayed on the side."

"Did you meet any of Doris' children?"

"I had mentioned that Doris's older daughter had passed away shortly before she returned to work. She had only two daughters, and I had the opportunity to meet her other daughter. Doris was a real person with a great heart. She was my angel for a while."

10 – The Purchase of My House was a Miracle

"A woman with her two girls and a boy lived in one of those apartments. Her rental situation was similar to mine; we both had three children excepting that she had two girls and a boy, and I had two boys and a girl. I learned that the apartment manager gave her the same agreement she gave us. Her children stayed alone in the apartment complex playing after school hours until she returned from work; this woman worked during the day. Tenants complained that her children made excessive noise in the playground. Tenants said her children ran around the complex screaming and yelling, and shook the enclosed swimming pool fence. A few days later, the manager sent out a letter to all tenants; she requested them to sign a *petition to evict* the woman and her three children. We did not sign that letter because we judged it unjust. The playground rules allowed children of all ages to play and have fun in the playground area within the family complex. We had a right of letting our children and pets in that family area per the rental agreement. The manager did what she wanted to do; she pleased certain single tenants in that family area. She evicted that family and turned around to threaten us. I knew she wanted to get rid of us no matter what; and she began performing frequent inspections of our apartment looking for grounds for eviction; it was sad but true. My children did not play in the playground; they stayed in the apartment after school. I worked across the street, and I had better control on that situation. How good that was; I realized the broad benefits I got out of my company's moving to across the street from my apartment.

"The pressure and the fears grew to the point that my husband and I decided to look for another place. My husband came home from work one afternoon calling me, excited. 'Misti', he yelled scaring me; I did not know what was happening. He said, 'I saw a house, a man, the housekeeper, let me in to see the inside and the backyard. I asked him if I could bring you to see it in an hour, and he said yes, he would show the house gladly. Do you want to go?' It came to my mind in an instant, 'how are we going to see a house if we cannot afford to buy it?' Nevertheless, we went to see the house together. It was a nice small house as the one in the Cinderella's tale, I said. Later when we entered, the man showing the house told us that it was a Cinderella model. The house had three bedrooms, two full baths, a formal living room, kitchen and dining area, a family room and had ample land to extend it. It had a large back yard with flower plants and grass, a front yard with San Agustin grass, everything looked well taken care of. The man told us that it had several months in the listing, but nobody had come to see it until now. By curiosity, I asked him what was the selling price, and he hand out a flyer with the price and the photo of the house. The man suggested us to call the real estate agent to get more information on the sells terms and conditions.

"The house was nice; I liked it since I saw it; however, I did not see how we could qualify with a bank for financing. Rangel called the agent, Phyllis, two or three days after our visit, and arranged an appointment with her for the coming Friday. We went to our appointment after we returned from work that Friday; Phyllis solved all finance, loan, and the title process questions in the application, and closed the loan in fewer than four hours. Do you remember my story of the car we bought? The purchase of this house was just like that. I could not come out of my astonishment; it was so easy that it scared me, and thrilled me so much that my whole body shook. I had cold sweats coming and going because of my fears and the uncertainties of that moment. Phyllis and Rangel filled out paper forms, and I did not know if I should laugh or cry because of my nerves.

"Buying this house was the maximum that could happen to us; even though this house was the third real estate property we had bought. What happened was unbelievable; it was like a dream of which I did not want to wake up before it came true. I was already thinking about the remodeling we could do to that house; but at the same time, I knew the responsibility we got. The minutes were ticking away, eternal minutes they were, and I was scared to wake up out of this dream; however, the voices, the papers, the signatures, all were shouting at me, wake up, this is not a dream, and if it were, it had come true. They close the deal; Phyllis prepared a package of documents for us that we took. I wanted to get out that office quickly; I did not wanted to give any opportunity of recalling the process we completed for any detail left out. We arrived at the apartment, and we continued talking about how easy it was to buy our house. The emotion of that moment was so much that I was not listening to Rangel speaking. He tried to say something to me that did not hear. He said a rental clause included in the purchase documents allowed us to rent that house for the days the escrow process took to close and deliver the deed; so, we could move in right away. The next day in the morning, we notified the apartment manager that we would terminate our rental agreement at the end of its contractual term in seven days; it was safe for us to do that because the loan was bank guaranty."

"Was that case another non-standard procedure; do you think? Could you explain what you think happened? Was it the work of the angels in your way?"

"For me, the angels managed the whole set of circumstances and manipulated the end result; I have no doubts. Let me come back to your question later on, I want to continue my story saying that we rented the house right away; the bank had approved the loan the Monday following the paper signing, and we moved in the house a few days later but less than a week. We returned the apartment keys to the manager at the last hour of the last day of that rental agreement. Going back to your question, I say that I went through many days thinking about the flow of circumstances that occurred to conclude that purchase; how could all this had happened if my husband had steady employment for a little less than two years, and I had just over two years since I started mine? I thought we did not have a chance to qualify; we had not enough time at work to consider it a steady employment. We had a small balance in our bank account and had no credit established at that time; nevertheless, the application had no obstacles. I have no doubts that my angels managed the circumstances of that purchase, and made the requirements easier for us to buy that house."

"How did the angels manage the circumstances; what did they do?"

"With that in mind, I asked my husband, 'what made you go to that neighborhood? Had you seen that house before?' He said, 'I had not, Misti, I had not seen that house before'. He continued, 'I had an urge to enter that urban development area; this house was the first thing I saw as I went in for a couple of blocks into that development. I did not see any *for rent* signs around, and when I saw the house for sale sign, immediately, I stopped and got out the car. I saw nobody around that house, but after a few minutes, a man came out of the little side gate next to the garage with a shovel and a broom. He looked at me as if he were calling me, and I walked toward him; I spoke with him, and the rest is history you know already'. The story Rangel told me reaffirmed my belief in that this was my guardian angels work; they managed the circumstances to make possible the purchase of that house. Rangel went by his spontaneous impulses and reactions; he did not think about going in that day. He entered that urban development as taken by the hand according to him; he did not see anything else because straight away he saw that house. This event was something as if that house called him, 'Rangel, come see me. I am here waiting for you.' It was as if a magnet attracted him to the site. One could say my assessment was an exaggeration; however, one could not deny the process was rapid and the result came out in our favor. I think, in a normal case, a house purchase agreement goes through a slow, calm, and painstaking process that takes several weeks. In our case, it was not like that; they waved, avoided, or adjusted the qualification requirements so we may buy that house. I think my yearning to find a place where we could move as soon as possible triggered a chain of events; I saw three angels, Rangel, the housekeeper man, and, Phyllis, the real estate agent, acting in this story. For me, this bizarre sequence of events in this episode was the work of my guardian angels, and nothing else. One may say that it was a struck of luck and others might say it was God's blessing; however, the end result shows the definite purpose of providing a place where we could live in peace within the short time we had left in that apartment rental agreement. We receive all the benefits at the end of this episode.

11 – How I Bought the Other Vehicle

"We would need to buy a car for our daughter, who was coming to driving age. We did neither tell anybody we needed one nor we had started to look for one; however, there it was. Mister Chuck offered us one. Let me tell how this happened; One day, Mister Chuck, my boss at work, asked me if we needed another car. I answered him that I did not know, but I would ask my husband. He explained that his mother had bought a car, but she stopped driving it because of her health conditions. He said that if we wanted it we could come to see it at her mother's house. I was shocked with surprise, he offered us a car that indeed we would need. He did not know that but we needed a car for our daughter. I asked, 'oh! My god is this another deed of my angels? They are acting one-step ahead of our needs, or it seemed.' We, of course, went to see the car; it was new with fewer than 3,200 driven miles, new tires, impeccable interior still smelling as new, and it looked as if it had not driven at all. We bought the car, but we did not drive it much, in fact, until my daughter got her driver's license, and we gave it to her. This car came at the right time and without us neither looking for it nor telling anybody, we need it. I thought that Plymouth car was a gift from Mister Chuck, because in fact the value of the car was higher than the amount we paid for. Mister Chuck's kindness created in me an immense gratitude; I thought I had to pay back with a good deed onto others. This was another story of my experiences with guardian angels in my way that came to take care of me. For me, Mister Chuck was an angel in my way; otherwise, at least, he was the instrument that my angels used in order for me to get that car.

"That car we bought was indeed a farewell gift from Mister Chuck; he retired; by this time, I had overcome my fear of handling my work, and I had significantly improved my knowledge and experience of office procedures. In fact, I was the office administrator for more than two years before he retired. I remember many things of Mister Chuck, but the one that comes first to my mind is my interview with him back in 1981 when I applied for that job. Although I had some work experience, I had been away for work a long time; but I died of nervousness and fears. It was obvious that I did not meet the job requirements, considering the interview results; but he gave me the job anyway. I remember that I almost quit that job, but I stayed thanks, in part, to his encouragement and trust for which I could not fail him."

12 – Beginning of a calm and peaceful time

"Misty, I sense that you and your family had settled down, can you explain that condition?"

"Yes, Miguel, I felt that we settled down right after we bought that house. I still work for that insurance company. The children grew up and went on to make their own life. My parents stayed there in my native country, and they received my attention. My sister went her own way and my brother stayed with my parents in my house, in that country. I kept my friendships with Mitza, Doris, and Aida, and our lives went by with no major difficulties.

"We think we will not leave America again; we have no place to go if it is not for a short vacation. We know there is no country besides the United States offering steady comfort and peace. Our native country offers nothing besides grief and despair; nevertheless, we do not know what life hold in the future. I tried to bring my family from my native country to America. I retained a law firm to get their permanent visa five years after I had returned to America. This was my own endeavor and my angels did not intervene. I thought that these actions were outside of my angels concerns. Nevertheless, I had my doubts because in some way it could be that I prepared the threads to tie this event in the future. I was doing it out of love for my family and my desired that they live in the comfort and peace, this country offered. These efforts did not work as I expected; perhaps, I did not consider all the conditions required to make my wish reality. I think the angels did not include this family proximity in the plan they followed. At the end of this passage, only my sister and her two sons decided to live in America. My brother came to study in America, but he had no desire to live here. He studied and got his pilot license, and then returned to that country. My parents wanted to come only for a visit whenever I brought them, and they decided to live in that country. I thought for a while about what went wrong and why I could not accomplish my wish. I think I was dealing with individuals who had their own interests and preferences I could not control; and I learned that the angels could have accomplished my desire because they can see the future and read those individual's minds. These circumstances were not as complex as the circumstances of my other stories. For these reasons, I said my angels managed them to produce desired results. My family story was sad; it showed how a family broke up and chose to spread across several countries; it lost its beauty and family unity. I knew each one of them had the right to choose and decide; their choices matched none of my intention, and I wondered why my efforts came out that way. I said it must be for a definite purpose that I failed to observe. I confirmed that when my decisions, actions, or their results broke the purpose of my mission, the angels intervened to bring me back on course.

13 – The Continuous Caring for My Parents

"We may not say why things happen with absolute certainty; one may explain the physical phenomenon, how and when it happened. For instance, why did I rush to my native country before the big earthquake? I am sure that events always occur for a purpose. Now, at my age, I see that my parents needed my support and attention more and more each day since that earthquake; and that the sole responsibility of providing them with comfort for the rest of their life subtlety grew in me with time. Rangel has been the leading angel of my mission; because, instead of opposing me, he has offered me all the support I needed for helping my parents. I always thought my turn would come some day when I would understand my mission in life, and with pleasure, I would fulfill it. I finally understood that my mission was to care for my parents.

"My parents had gone through many perils; since that earthquake destroyed their house, the economic situation when my father no longer worked, forced him to sell his house. They did have neither a place to move nor anybody to help them in their needs. At that time, I assumed the responsibility of helping them, and I began to care for them. I moved them to my house in that country and took over the cost of their living. No one in my family could care for my mother, my brother, and my house in my native country. I have fulfilled this responsibility expecting no rewards; I had done what I had to do when required. For me, it was obvious, that this was the mission of my life, and I feel proud and honored that God had assigned it to me."

Misti paused for a moment as to hold her emotion privately. She was emotionally touched, and her tears rolled down on her cheeks. I said, "Would you like to take a break?" She took her glass of water from the table, drank, and with quivering voice she said, "No, I am OK;" and she continued.

"My situation is not easy, Miguel; my father passed away three years ago. My brother had a surgery to stop damage to his spinal cord; he is now partially handicapped. My mother sickness advances with time. My brother still lives with my mother taking care of her in my house, in that country. For me, my brother is an angel in my way; he has been attentive to my mother's needs disregarding mutual personal differences they have. My brother is a little hand extended and prepared to make the last ties in the embroidering of my life."

"Misti, why did you decided to let your parents live in your native country? Would had not been better for them and you to have them closer to you, here in America?"

"That was my parents' choice, and I understood that. My parents decided to stay in my house, in that country to avoid grievances adjusting to this scenario at their age. They did not speak English and had to depend on me for everything, and I understood that. They were right; I needed to work each day here in America, and it would have been extremely difficult for me to care and tend for my sick and aging parents. Perhaps, I would not have had sufficient resources to place them in private care here in America; but, caring, and attending my parents' needs requires resources I can afford there, in my native country."

"Well, it seems that you have reached the plateau of your commitments. Is there anything you anticipate happening? Can you tell us?"

"I have had no significant experiences with my guardian angels since the day we purchased the house. It seems that a long lasting calm has settled in my life. The embroidering of my life is not yet finished; other events may still come and the weaving will advance to its completion. I feel that what may come could be nothing more than endeavoring to maintain my pace to the end of my mission. By now, thirty years have gone by since I returned to the United States. In addition, during this time, I have been taking care of my parents with no difficulties."

14 – My Mother's Health Situation

"Misti, how can you take care of your parents and your brother not being there in your native country? How can you do that while taking care of your immediate household?"

"Many things have happened related to my mission during that calm I mentioned. For instance, for some reason I am not aware of, Aida decided to go back to our native country, one day. It was strange move because she was doing well in America; she had a steady job as a certified nurse. Her four sons had moved out and were living on their own. Aida still had her house in her native country rented to dependable tenants; so, it was not because of that. She did not have a job waiting for her there; so, it was not that either. In the end, Aida sold her furnished condominium and went back to her native country. She left alone leaving behind her four boys in America. She went back a few months before my father died; and my mother health started to deteriorate. She may have had her own reasons for going back, but her relocations happened in time to help me with my father. Out of her free will, Aida began helping my mother, since my father's funeral. I see that Aida's returned to my native land had helped me; and now, she is assisting my mother and my brother on her own time and possibilities. When I study her move in more detail, I see an exact timing of events; and I concluded that the angels were behind her story in connection with mine as well. She is attentive of my mother's condition, and in fact, she does what I would do if I were there with my mother. Aida has no obligation to help me. She gets no benefit from her attentions with my mother. For me, Aida is an Angel in my way who has not yet fulfilled her entire mission with respect to my life. It is not for me to believe that I am the center of the universe where everything moves about of me. It is better for me to believe that each one of us has a mission to accomplish. I found some individuals, that I called agents, who have helped me with accomplishing my mission as part of their missions. I have collaborated with their missions for the same reason. I thought that the angels had used these agents on activities that helped me with accomplishing my mission.

"Where do you place Aida in your life?"

"She is a great friend. My relation with Aida was different from others with respect to the mission my life. She was different from Mitza for instance. Mitza's activities were clear and explicit, short and light, and at the end of her, she continued on her own way. Recalling Manuel, I saw his function as evident, specific, easy, and abrupt in relation to my life; and then he continued on his way leaving no tracks behind in the end. On the other side and closer to my family, I saw my brother; he continues near my mother representing me. Maybe my sister should be the one, instead of Marcus, who should care for my mother; but that is not the prevailing situation, and my brother dedicated himself to oversee my mother's care. My brother is, for me, the other angel in my way. Why do I say that? Let us see, my brother, as my sister, had the choice to go on an independent way or to remain to care for my mother until she left us; but he is there taking care of my mother. It is not easy to care for a sick person when that person needs permanent assisted living. Marcus made his choice and was there for that reason. I am here working to support them both and the house. How could I not thank and admire him for what he does? How could I not give him the credit of being, if not the instrument, an angel in my way? For now, Miguel, I have no more stories to tell even though I have many other real life experiences. Nevertheless, what I have narrated is the main flow of events that draw my mission. The missing stories will come up ahead in the manner that threads are still waiting to tie at last in the embroidering of my life. This means that any extended waiting hands meet other hands to make the final connections. At that time, and only at that time, the picture on the embroidering of my life will reach its conclusion. Therefore, I hope that I had given you in my stories the information you needed to finish your book."

Chapter 11

Misti's Conclusions and Recommendations

"Wait, Misti, please, wait. Still we have not finished this interview. Some issues remain without an explanation."

"Tell me now, why waiting. I have given you my time and the time remaining is short."

"The stories described the angels in your way, do they exist?

Is the picture that the threads weave in the embroidering of your life clear? Is there any time to answer those questions?"

1 – Who has Authority on the Angels Subject?

"What kind of questions are these? Miguel, what questions?

"I say that I am not the best person to judge on this issue. I am just a witness telling the stories of my lifetime experience. I would let the readers to study the evidences I present and reach their own conclusions. Tell me, what can my saying that they exist or not contribute to the proof of their existence? The cynicism of human beings gives little space for discussing the subject of the angels in my way. I know there are persons as I, living in silence for years hiding their experiences. The world would never know about these experiences if nobody comes out to tell his or her stories. These experiences would forever remain sealed in the minds of the witness. In this world, we must prove the evidences with objective means and methods; we cannot express spiritual things. We live under some sort of rules of manmade laws; and the spiritual experiences may turn inadmissible in the judgment of men. I accepted that we lived on the brink of risk; however, the situations yield risks. The circumstances or the combinations of these can change the risks they carry. My stories have demonstrated the risks and obstacles that in some way the angels resolved. For me, the greatness of this mystery is that although the circumstances were against me in most cases, the results came in my favor. I answered yes; I have the time to answer the last questions without reservations. Because having told my real life experiences, your book would be incomplete if I do not explain the reasons of my beliefs, I think. Your book would be incomplete if my narrations did not have a synopsis of the stories I have told. That is, a fundamental map of my experiences; the picture still weaving in the embroidering of my life."

2 – The Spiritual Dimension of the Angels

"Do angels exist? Where do they live?"

"I have no doubts about guardian angels going by my experiences, but that's my mind set. Nevertheless, I have experienced an energy around us that is not physical; but it transcends into our physical world. I think that if this energy is not part of the physical world; then, it part of a spiritual dimension that we do not access at will. Strange things go on in life; and by that I mean life seen and unseen. This spiritual energy comes to us in the form of physical actions that we perceive or in thoughts that we conceive. This energy could come to us in the form of the action of a person or of an animal, or it could come from environment influence; but these direct our activities in a different path. I think that my theory is correct; and my stories showed the manifestation of that energy acting on my behalf. I considered that this energy is an expression of love that cares for us. We know we live in a real world where we get experiences through the senses; but we are not limited to sensing because we think. I have said that perceptions come into the mind, and we retain copies of the reality in our memories. We make images from bits of perceptions, and we store them in our memories as knowledge of our experiences. We build knowledge from our concepts in our minds that become reality. I know that these images have no form, weight, or volume in our memory; they become intangible and invisible to us in the physical world. We cannot longer prove that what we recall exists if the real object does not exist anymore. People take the story we tell when they think it is logically possible; but in any case, it remains as hearsay. The meaning of our words and the words we hear remain as images in our memories. The meanings include both conceptions and perceptions no matter where they come from. My own experiences of the action of the angels support their existence. Most religions believe that angels exist, and I agree with that. I am convinced that angels are in a world we cannot access physically; but angels cannot show themselves in our physical world; they cannot form part of physical circumstances or events as the spirits that they are. Nevertheless, the angels' actions have a purpose just as words have a meaning. The action of an angel, as the meaning of a word, has intensity, a direction, and a purpose. I think of words as elements of a notion or a thought; so, I accept the angels as spiritual forces transcending into our physical dimension. They come through notions and perceptions. My experiences say that angels, as force, act in and out of man's minds; and they seem to manipulate whole sets of circumstances, mental and psychical. I have said that the angels had transformed conditions and circumstances to get definite results at the end of each story. Based on this, I say the angels incited my mother's thoughts to insist with zeal that I learned that language; however, her insistence always was beyond her awareness. The purpose was to prepare me to live in America. The angels prepared the conditions that made my life and studies possible in that country. Who would have known that by learning English I would have made my living smooth with no significant problems in that country? I will not forget that after I had gone back at the end my studies I thought that my destiny was to remain in my country; but the angels did manage the conditions there and made it easy for me to return to America. I knew that through my working in the United States I was preparing myself to fulfill my mission. I had explained that the angels forced me to return to my native country with no logical reasons before that earthquake. I found out a few weeks later that it was for a single purpose, supporting and helping my parents during and after that earthquake. A short time after that cataclysm, I saw the purpose and the value of that rushed return. When the situation had normalized, other forces changed the circumstances to expel us out of that country; we went to a neighboring country. I saw that the neighboring country served as springboard or transit station on our way back to America. It was clear to me that the angels managed the situations in the neighboring country. They turn it hostile and we had no other choice than leaving that country as soon as possible; we returned to the United States once again. Once in America, I saw how other angels or the same in different forms helped me gain employment a couple of weeks after we came back. I found that the angels managed the circumstances so we could rent that apartment. I saw how the angels worked the circumstances to provide items and furnishings for my apartment in a short time. I saw how the angels rushed us into buying a car, a house, and a second car. I saw my company relocate to that place across the street from my apartment;

I did not see a clear justification. I did not doubt that the angels had managed the conditions that forced the relocation of my company; so, I did not have to drive that long distance to my previous work place. Now, at the end of my narratives, I am sure that the angels created the conditions for me to care and support my aging parents. It was a long chain of events that built the path in my life; it was a deterministic plan of action linked and leading to fulfill my mission. This was the entire purpose of my life, to prepare myself and assume a solid position to care for them; it was the mission of my life. I am here in America, and they, my mother and my brother, remained in my house there in my native country. I love my parents and my brother, and it does not matter what sacrifice I must make to give them a decent living conditions. I thank my husband for understanding that I had to care for my parents as they aged; without him, perhaps I would not be able to care for them. As a final point, I want to summarize my narratives; I want to display the final picture weaved in the embroidering of my life. I want to say; however, that my embroidering still has certain threads remaining lose that will tie in the future. When the angels make these final ties the embroidering of my life will be complete, and you may frame it and hang it on a wall I want to indicate. 'Do you know, Miguel?' I want this book to be the frame of my embroidering and by publishing it; you hang it on the wall of existence. This way, the world will have an opportunity to see how the angels guide me to accomplish the mission God had chosen for me. I am positive that there are people who have experiences like mine that they could share; however, they may have neither interest nor courage to tell their experiences to the public. I was like them, but I realized that my experiences were real. I did not make up all these events and the logical sequence, in which they happened. My stories were real life experiences written in the history of my life. To answer your question, and by my experiences, I say that the angels in my way exist. They will travel with me until the air I breathe is no longer available."

3 – Two Relative Dimensions: Spiritual and Material

"Let me ask one last question. Is this OK?" I said, 'Thank you,' after Misti accepted nodding politely."

"What can you tell us about this spiritual dimension you mentioned?"

4 – What are Spirit and Mater?

"I am the wrong person to take on that issue, Miguel. My scanty studies do not let me find proof of spiritual realities. You may find other qualified persons who can explain your concerns clearer. I can tell, however, about my own experiences and about what I deduce from them. You may see the messages and actions of the angels. It is necessary to release the prejudices that do not let us see that. I mentioned that in your mindset, Miguel, you might have no place for spiritual issues that I tell in my stories. I think, however, that deep in your soul you may think the angels may be real; otherwise, I see no purpose for your desire to hear and write my experiences. I think that by telling my stories and explaining their results I help to prove the angels interactions. I know that we have no physical methods to capture the angels' interactions with us. These interactions show up with no warning; they appear as part of the activity sequence of an event. Let us keep in mind the filters – our prejudices - of our minds I mentioned. With this, filters opened; let us look for the angels and their messages in future experiences by others or in our own experiences. The spiritual experiences are unique and particular; only those who lived them will keep them in their memories. The experiences in a story, if told, expose evidences to the scrutiny of sciences, beliefs, or faiths. My thought is simple; if we accept to discuss the issue of angels, we accept the possibility of their interaction with us, do you agree?"

"Yes, I think that is a fair conclusion."

5 – How Misti explains Destiny and Luck

"In my stories, I tried to tell that life is a complete network of events that happen for a definite purpose. It is as an embroidering on which I knit the image of the mission God assigned me at birth. It is a network or mesh with all its nodes, crossings, and moorings the weaving the embroidering with the picture of the mission of my life. The yarn, strings or threads, their colors, the pattern in which they overlay shape the picture of my mission on that embroidering in the end. We need to know that if we have a mission in life this implies that destiny is, in fact, the end of that mission and not the intermediate points. In this case, I had the right to choose while I traveled along the path taking me to the end, my mission; however, I do not have the faculty to choose my mission. It appears that, I was free to choose what I wanted within the boundaries, across the width, of the road of my life, as long as my choices did not destroy the course to accomplish my mission. It seems that I can make choices and decisions from one side to the other, across my road, without going out of the road while we go forward on my way. Free will enabled me to choose the steps on my way because it is what I wanted to do. My steps occurred in a set order in my stories, regardless, if I wanted them or not. Therefore, destiny is not a set of predefined steps that I must take in my way. Destiny is whatever it may be in the end or the end itself. Accordingly, I can only see my destiny at the time I get to the end of my way. In other words, my destiny does not mark the steps of my walk, but walk marks my destiny at the end of it. What is destiny? People believe that it is a chain of events that we cannot change. They say that it is inevitable and out of our control. For me, it is the end of a purpose. Is it fate? I do not think so. According to some people, fate is a force that irresistibly acts on men and events. For me, destiny is the final picture completed in the embroidering of my life, my mission.

"I spoke of the angels in my way as apparent forces that influence material circumstances and minds of people. I spoke of a fixed mission at the end of the integration of all the events in the embroidering of my life. Therefore, I agree with you when you say that, 'We live subject to circumstances, at the brink of risks, in a probabilistic world.' We have no intermediate destiny because we can choose at will along our way; but we cannot choose our end. Our destiny is the final destination we reach when we complete the mission of our lives. Therefore, our destiny is the completed mission; the actions that we take to reach the end depend on the decisions we make within the circumstances we face. Always, thinking that we are in charge, we make the decisions within the circumstances present at that time. There are those who combine destiny with luck, and I think that luck is a basic term that defines the result of random action. I saw that luck comes from random and accidental circumstances that are out of our control. I have seen that causal circumstances have no specific purpose; I have seen that destiny has no middle ends. This is due to their random nature that makes then casual."

6 – How Misti sees Spiritual - Mater Transcendence

"How do angels transcend into our real world?"

"When we talk about angels, we talk about entities of a spiritual nature that we do not know. Our problem is that we do not have understanding of their nature and of the instruments or devices that the angels use to transcend into our world. We do not have the tools to communicate with them in their spiritual dimension. I think that the angels talk to us using a silent language and manage our thoughts and the situations in our world to give us just the option they want us to take. They do this because they are spirits; they are invisible and intangible. Angels cannot touch or grasp anything material; they have no shape, weight, or volume. If we want to study a spiritual dimension, then we must include its border line and our world. Our interest is to know how and where the angels cross that borderline into our world. We can only perceive what happen up to that borderline; this is where the potential encounters with the angels (spirits) starts. For me, that is it. From generations people have preserved the belief that a spiritual dimension exists, and spirits live there. These spirits transcend into our world for whatever purposes they may have. Certain religions preach that there is a place called heaven where spirits live."

7 – What are indeed The Angels' Roles?

"Misti, can you distinguish the roles of the angels in your way?"

"Let me say, the angels act as facilitators of my welfare. They manage the options available in my way for my choosing. They manage the circumstances and conditions that yield a desired result, and ensure that we chose, decide, and act to get our mission done. In addition, as you heard in my stories, the angels do not choose on my behalf; I am who makes the choices by way of the angels' arrangement of circumstances they present to me. Let us assume that they do not manipulate the circumstances. The conditions still force me to take the choice that offers me the maximum benefit for my purposes. I do not know of anybody that wants to take less than what a situation offers him or her. Thus, I accept that we live subject to the circumstances manipulated or not by the angels in our way. Remember that case of the dog that made me decide to skip the last step to death; think well, the dog did not decide for me, I decided to skip the step and the result was different, avoiding the collision with the vehicle. The circumstances of the scenario, the risks, and dangers that my husband and family went through in my native country did not decide for us; we took the best way out available at that time. The economic situation of that country did not decide for us either; it just became hostile to the point that we had to leave. We decided to go back to USA; here we would have continuous security and peace. Here we would have many opportunities to succeed in life and in my mission. In spite of the preparation of the circumstances, you see, we still have free will.

"It did not matter for us then how the circumstances or combinations channeled the actions. It did not matter indeed how the events had occurred; for us the results counted. The basic points were that the angels provided viable options for us to choose. As I have said, the walk does not determine our destiny, but the end of the walk. We may add that the circumstances do not typifies an event, but the result of the combination of these. I may say that the event produced a result that was more than the sum of the contribution of each one of these circumstances. Perhaps you were right when you said, 'we live subject to the circumstances;' however, the angels managed the circumstances to yield the results that marked the events supporting my mission. The angels managed the circumstances to gain set purposes as we have seen in my stories. This was not what we thought of probabilistic events in this world; our notion is that random circumstances combine in the events and define their result in this world. I learned that a change of the circumstances inevitably changed the result. The result depends on how the angels managed the circumstances. It is as taking out certain numbers before playing a bingo game; the numbers we took out bias the result. On the one hand, when the missing numbers affects the bingo cards other than mine, I have higher chance of winning. In the other hand, the more numbers we take out that do not affect my bingo card the greater is my probability of winning.

"The law of cause and effect implies the dependency of events; by consequence, the purpose of an event happening now is to serve as the base for another event to happen in the future. Well, let us think. I said that a current event depended in one or more events completed, and waited to support future events. The key issue is that an event showed its purpose when it prepared to wait for its connection with other event in the future. It was exciting for me to see, therefore, the purpose of a connection. I think that the global plan for the embroidering of my life has a defined general purpose; and what the angels do is arrange the circumstances to produce the wished results. Let us think that nobody changes the circumstances and let the circumstances occur at random; we will see that the concept of ties waiting for future connections does not matter. Random events have random results, and these results have no defined purpose. Furthermore, in this case the threads left hanging loose in the embroidering may or may not have a future tie. In fact, it does not matter for them if they connect or not. The ties would be messy, and the image weaved on the embroidering may not give a defined figure but a deformed picture with no sense at the end of the weave. This is not what we have seen in my stories because I have put in evidence the purpose of each event in the sequence.

8 – Angels are Reality not Suppositions.

"I want to say something on your doubts about the angels, and give me a few minutes more in this interview, do you agree?" Misti noted.

"Yes, of course, Misti, this is your interview, please go ahead."

"You asked, 'are angels, fact, or belief?' Well, do you remember that phrase that says, *'Nothing is true, nothing is lie, everything is according to the color of the glass that look,' Ramon Campoamor y Campoosorio, Navia, Asturias 1987.* "Indeed, everything depends on the vantage point from where we look. For me, the crystal through which I look is the mental, emotional, or physical conditions that an angel may give at the time we get a message. I know that, even the same person could see a different view of the same subject, object, or circumstance if the conditions change. I saw that the results were independent of the conditions that I faced at the time of my experience with the angels. How may I confirm that angels appearing in my way exist or not? Perhaps, we never prove their existence, if what we want is a picture of the angels to show they are reality; it is not possible. The angels are not mater. The reality is that the physiognomy of the angels should not be our concern; and we should concern ourselves with their actions and the purpose of their actions. They say that the words are a measure with deeds, and the law of causality covers the cause and effect. The stories I told for your book always presented a result; this result defined its basis and causes, as evidences of the circumstances causing the result. Causes are necessary; however, in the end of a story, the result is what counts. In my story, what matters is getting to the end. Remember the philosophical concept *'the end justifies the means,' The Prince, Nicolo Machiavelli, 1532?"*It implies that anything is acceptable if it is to achieve an end. This is not applicable to my stories because the results were not forced; these were free and consistent with the justice of the Creation.

"I have shown in my stories that each result served as a basis, and support of other events concluded later. In a series of events, the current events depend on one or some past events; and any subsequent events depend on the present events. Think about it; it is impossible to construct a house building the roof with no framing, building the frame with no foundations. We build that house following a forward sequence; life is a forward sequence of events. In my stories, I demonstrated that some events chained with mine weaved the history of my life. If my life were certain, the decisions I make were certain in each event. I learned that the conditions, reasons, and impulses served as the basis of my decisions. Thus, by observing these elements I sensed the making of the events in my stories. The messages that the angels sent were physical parts of my decisions. These angels always gave me clear physical results and for my benefit. I will let the readers of your book get their own conclusions from my stories because they have the right to believe or not the reality of my experiences. Nevertheless, I think, that if the readers had experiences as mine, he or she could find at least in his life the messages of the angels of their way; they may conclude, as I did, that the angels exist in the form they choose for each set of circumstances."

9 – *Misti explanations of the Embroidering of her Life*

9.1 – *Synopsis of My Mission*

"Misti, can you summarize all you have said in your stories?"

"Yes, Miguel, but to conclude, let me explain the resemblance of the embroidering with the mission of my life, is it OK?"

"Go ahead, Misti, and take your time."

"In that case, let me begin by creating an outline of the content of the embroidering of my life. By now, it is obvious that the mission of my life was to care, protect, and support my parents.

"I needed that certain conditions were in place for me to provide them with care, according to my experiences; this was in a long process beginning at my childhood. My stories show, the angels' endeavors focusing on a place from where I could mobilize to assist and help my parents. It had to be a place where I could return upon completing my assignments. I showed in my stories circumstances and events that were methodically changing the course of my life. It was as weaving the threads of the embroidering of my life to accomplish, one by one, the required conditions. I list five crucial conditions I needed to satisfy are as follows.

        "A –   Personal Preparation - I had to prepare myself to live in a free, stable, safe place, and for which I had to dominate the English language.

        "B –   Place of Residence - I had to obtain permanent residence in the selected place.

        "B1-   Mobility -I needed time to go away, assist my parents and come back when no longer needed.

        "C –   Continuous Resources - I needed a continuous source of income and resources to afford their needs.

        "C1 – I had to have a permanent and reliable employment.

        "C2 – Back up - I had to have a source of income and support back up.

        "D –   Housing - I had to have a place for my parents to stay in my native country.

        "E –   Additional Support - I had to have personal back up in my native country."

"I am impressed by the way you have outlined the journey of your life. Can you break down the chain of events around those five major goals?"

"Now, forty years since that big earthquake, and at the end of my stories, I see the content of the drawing in the weave of the embroidering of my life. I had listed some conditions that needed to happen for me to accomplish my mission. I found twenty-one major conditions in my mission that I had to accomplish to get to this point. It is a summary of what I said in my stories; I pointed out the moorings of the weaving that made the embroidering.

        "1 - I study English in my country, but it was too slow and insufficient.

        "2 – I maintained my friendship with Mitsa because she was the bridge for me to travel to America and study English.

        "3 – Alina moved to USA to wait for me when I was ready to go to that country.

"4 –   Roger appeared in my life; and a friendship with him created a threatening situation that forced my parents into thinking that it was best to send me away from him.

"5 –   The parents of Mitza convinced my parents to let me go to finish my studies in America.

"6 -   I went to America to finish my studies and at the same time to set up certain connections I needed ahead.

"7 –   Rangel appeared in my life and provided me with his company.

"8 –   I married Rangel, and he took me back to USA, completing the tie left waiting in USA. He was the companion in my life and potential resource back up I will need.

"9 -   I settled down and I got my first employment in America. This employment gave me the basic job history I would need in the future.

"10 –   I rushed to my native country to assist, support and care for parents before and after that massive earth quake.

"11 –   I had to live a hostile situation so I could get out of my native country with no regrets. A neighboring country was the host for my move. I wanted to stay as close as possible to my parents. That country was not the scenario in which I needed to be, but it was the fastest and easiest way to get away from my native country.

"12 –   I needed to have help in America to ease my return. Aida had moved to America with her children and waited for my return ready to lend me a hand.

"13 –   I had to be in a safe and prosperous place as America. The neighboring country turned into a hostile scenario and forced me to go back to USA.

"14 –   I had to return to the state from where I had lived before. My husband employment fails in that southern state. I found out that Aida had moved to America, and she offered her house in that western state.

"15 –   I moved to that western state to join Rangel, and my children a couple of weeks later.

"16 –   I had to have a permanent job. Aidas's husband helped me to find a job with the insurance company he worked.

"17 –   I needed to establish a strong income source. Rangel got a job with a manufacturing company two months after I got mine; that established the stronger income source.

"18 –   I needed to secure my job. Doris came to train me in office procedures; and I avoided my resignation, my decision to quit my job.

"19 –   I needed to guarantee the place I settled in. I found all necessary conveniences in this western state; and I quickly established my permanent platform from where I would assist, support and care for my parents and brother.

"20 –   I needed to be calm and safe to accomplish my mission. My company moved to a building across the street from my apartment. I cut my stressful driving to my work. This condition allowed me to stay close to and spend some time with my children during my job lunch break.

"21 –   I necded to have a permanent place to operate at ease. The angels created the conditions for us to purchase our house.

"This is it, Miguel, now you can do as you please with this information."

"Thank you, Misti that is a thorough breakdown. I can follow the sequence of events now. Did you manage to settle in your house fast enough?"

"We were finally settled with all the conveniences and in our own house. We reached these conditions in time to start funding my aging parents' care on a continuous basis."

"What is happening now? How is your activity in relation to the angels in your way?"

"Twenty nine years have gone by since I return to America; we enjoy the calm and stability this country gives. The angels in my way have been inactive during this time, excepting perhaps minors incidents resolved; I have maintained the course of my mission. From this still transitory vantage point, I see the delta of the river of my life; and I see myself in the last backwater of this river flowing to its delta, slowly. I am at the end of my time when the golden waters of my river will discharge into to the sea of eternal existence. I think, however, that my mission has not yet come to its end. From this vantage point, I see the picture weaved on the embroidering of my life, the mission that God had assigned to me. Although I never requested this mission, and although I was not aware of it for a long time, it has been evident since long ago. Now my life is calm; I see the mission clearly, and I assume it resigned to resolve whatever difficulties might arise. Many years have gone by since I return to the United States, and nothing has changed. I care for my mother who needs ongoing assistance, and for my brother who is partly handicapped since years ago. I must take care of both of them in the mission chosen for me. They live now alone in my house, in my native land. I took care of my father until he died almost three years ago as part of my mission, fulfilled now. My father, my mother, and my brother had disagreements during the time when my father was still with us. In fact, they lived was a hopeless relationship. My sister, who lived and assisted my father in my house, in that country, during his last days, decided to go on her own way more of a year ago. My goal was to establish my position to assist, support and care for my parents. It had to be a free, in a rich country, where I had a comfortable life with sufficient resources to afford my parents care. My angels focused their endeavors to move me to America as I told in my stories. Here, I am attentive to my mission until it is over, because I will know when it is finally over, time wise."

10 – Misti advices to the Reader.

"Misti, would you like to give any advice to the readers of this book?"

"Miguel, I have no right to recommend the reader of this book what to believe or not. The readers have their own belief on this subject, even those who think that we live on the brink of risk, subject to circumstances in a probabilistic world. Nonetheless, I will suggest some ideas to the readers, but with no intention of telling them what to do or believe."

"Try, Misti, I think the readers expect some guidelines from this book. Could you do that?"

"Of course, I can; however, I still maintain that readers have the right to believe or not. I am no wizard to tell what to believe in. I will tell of the steps I used to open the filters of my soul and mind to capture the angels' manifestations and messages. Thus, let me say the following. Dear reader,

"Look for those events that change the course of your life and consider them with no fear.

"Open your mind and let it analyze your thoughts without prejudices the reasons of those events.

"Look for the sequence of those events and try to find their purposes, their connections, and moorings with other events in your past and future.

"When you find the sequence of those events, seek for the threads that weave, with all the characteristic, lines, and colors, the picture of the embroidering of your life.

"When that happens, you look for the angels in your way.

"Follow the signs of your angels' acts and you will find the plan through the circumstances yielding their objectives.

"Follow the path towards the lighthouse marking the harbor of the mission of your life.

"Record your experiences in a journal of your life.

"Maybe, someday, you will write the journey of your life, describing the picture on the embroidering of your life. I also, if I am still alive, can read your own stories with pleasure."

"Misti, I thank you. You gave an excellent and humble opinion; I did not expect anything less from you. You showy our deep understanding of the subject with a clear description in your stories."

"I told my stories, and I said I have no authority to force anybody to believe in angels. Those readers of your book who find evidences of events and results in their lives that came out in their favor without asking for it, can decide to believe or not. They have the right to declare that the existence of the angels in their way is true or absurd. Readers who find experiences similar to mine in their lives may see the embroidering of the mission of their lives.

"In my stories, I focused on current events that depend on past events and provide threads, links, and ties for coming events; nevertheless, at the same time, I focused on the weaving the embroidering of the mission of my life.

"Well, Miguel, my time is up. I thank you for the interest in the angels in my way. I hope my stories captured your interest, and answered your doubts. Now you can make an analysis of your own experiences, and if you do that, I hope you conclude and explain what you think about the existence of the angels in your way. Now, Miguel, that you lived my experiences in my stories, it is your turn to conclude if the angels exist. Therefore, if my experiences are real so are the angels. Moreover, I think that the stories I have told proved my experiences with angels. I will keep the conclusions I draw from my stories as evidence. I say again that the angels in my way exist, and they will continue to exist while I live.

"It has been a long day, but I enjoyed the interview and the opportunity to expose my experiences. I feel that I have unloaded a heavy weight off my shoulders and released the pressure in my chest. Thank you, God blesses you and good bye, Miguel."

Chapter 12

Writer's Notes

1 – Writer's Final Notes

"Thank you, Misti, you have been helpful and clear letting me into the intimacy of your beliefs. I ensure you that those who believe in guardian angels will appreciate the risk you took exposing your stories to the world. Those who seek real life experiences to support their own belief will gain from Misti's experiences. Those who are agnostic may find the glimpse of their reality in the experiences she has narrated. There is no doubt that the subject of this book, 'angels in my way,' is fascinating and inspiring. God blesses you and yours too. Misti got up slowly and invited me to follow her to the door. Indeed, it was a long, whole day, interview, but it was a rewarding experience. We shook hands and I left. Behind and still standing at the door, Misti was watching me walking away. I opened my car and look up to wave at Misti, but she was no longer there.

"As a writer, I agree with Misti that results are what count and not the integrated circumstances that make them. Misti is correct. I think that it is useless for us to spend time thinking about the way the circumstances integrate outside of our control. The people will always demand real proof of the angels' existence; they will take assumptions, nor hearsay, as evidences of their actions transcending into our world. I liked her concept of the two dimensions, the spiritual and material channel through which the angels come to our world. I liked the analogy of the angels' plan of actions to the weaving of strings on the embroidering of Misti's life. I appreciate how she described the chain of events weaving the picture of what she says is the mission in her life. I enjoyed her simple words and humble attitude towards my writing of the book of her experiences. She let the readers make their own decision about the existence of the angels; that impressed me a lot. She challenged the readers to search in their histories their own experiences; this was a way of requesting them to confirm by themselves their own belief. Perhaps, the education she received made her to respect the right of the people. She had advocated the freedom of choice under which people make their own choices and decisions.

"Misti's stories are real experiences of her life. Those stories showed circumstances and events that took her life on a definite path. People may have stories and can tell them, similar to Misti's stories. Perhaps, we may further explain the actions of the angels helping us in our world.

"Misti, we will remember you and your stories; as we will remember the strength of your character. Your convictions and that strength of character guarded your beliefs against hard the influences that challenged them in those days. That is the best example than you can give my readers. As for me, I lived your stories, and I will live them in my book repeatedly. I confess that, at certain moments, the words of your stories shook my own feelings and beliefs. For me, your combined stories are a story of love, real life experiences you have lived, of virtue and sacrifice. You have the love for your parents, your children, and husband. For that reason, I commend you and wish to give a poem that fixes what you think of the angels in your way as a tribute of your honesty and kindness; you have my eternal gratitude imbedded in the rime of that poem. Good bye, Misti, and God bless you, your parents, and your entire family."

To Misti for her courage telling her experiences

Angels in My Way

I

Phosphorescent reflexes of light
Through dimensions of my life Diffused.
Mysterious entities of the night
In twilight confused.

II

Sweet voices in subtle whispering
Of silent language unreal and dark,
Bringing a generous offering,
The energy that love sparks.

III

Oh! Transparent silhouettes rushed,
Rendered halo I have never asked,
Appealing, scary, subtle, and" blushed,
A strange intangible purpose masked.
Intensions that cannot be measured,
Is this your master plan assured?

IV

Infallible Conditions setters,
Altruistic angels in my way,
Are you Messengers that for better
Change and arrange things in my bay?

V

Do you ride at will my deed and thought
Along my life, my destiny you brought.
Then, if you are angels in my way,
Messengers of God's Peace and Goodness,
Twilight shadows I believe you may,
Fill the world with love not rudeness.

VI

Let me feel your ethereal presence,
Your messages in hours of my need,
The tender kindness in the essence
Of your trusted love and caring heed,
When? In your casual presence, albeit,
Whenever you wish to come... I will wait.
By, Miguel Angel Soto Flores, Stanton, CA August 19, 2010

www.ingramcontent.com/pod-product-compliance
Lightning Source LLC
Chambersburg PA
CBHW020513100426
42813CB00030B/3232/J